7 – 17
THE EXPERIENCE

7-17 THE EXPERIENCE

Keys to understand what is expected of
you in the future.

The book that is changing the perception of
how you have to prepare yourself for your career.

Glen Lapson

Publisher: Fundacion ECUUP

© 2015 Glen Lapson
www.glenlapson.com
Exclusive publishing rights
© 2017 Fundacion ECUUP.
Cinco de Marzo 16, planta 2, 50004, Zaragoza, Spain
www.fundacionecuup.org
English translation: Rose Marie Cartledge
Front Cover illustration: Joaquin Macipe

ISBN 978-84-949020-3-1

For you
who will never stop adding creative value

INDEX

CHAPTER 1

It is the end of the lesson. The teacher quickly goes over the work she has taught us today. She reminds us about what we should study for the following week. Immediately, there is a stir among my classmates. They're gathering papers and getting up from their seats. As always, I like watching what the teacher is doing. I remain seated for a while. It's not difficult to see her as I'm in the second row and my classmates sitting in the front row are doing the same thing.

The teacher carefully puts away the books she has open to follow the explanation, and inserts between the pages the two sheets of paper on which she has jotted down the questions that my classmate behind me has asked. She wants to study them at home because she finds the questions very interesting. My classmate is, of course, full of pride and, catching the mood of the rest of the class, I'm sure that he won't have any problem in asking again.

What I like most about this teacher is the way she puts away the pencils and pens she uses to make notes. She always arranges them in the same colour order: first the blue, then the red and finally the pencil. It is always the same routine. Always the same look of self-assurance. When she finally picks up her handbag, with a wide smile to the rest of the class, she stands up and as she walks to the door, she takes her leave, announcing: "In the next class, there will be more. I want you to practise everyday what we have learnt in today's lesson."

The truth is that I like this lady as my teacher. She cares about the students, making you feel important if you ask questions, and always tries to bring something new to the lesson. If only all teachers were as interesting! I hope the next teacher is as interesting.

Throughout the week at school, they have organised day activities intended, according to the teachers, to guide us in our future. I don't know if they realise that at 17 (many have already turned 18) the future for us is... in the future. We like to live in the present, to be together, experience life together and, above all, share what we're experiencing with each other. We say that the future will come. Although to be honest... No! The truth is that I don't think it will! I'm really worried.

It's Friday and for the last session of the day, they've organized a talk by someone who, they say, will tell us things about what awaits us. There's nothing to lose, just one more hour, then home, since it's Friday.

Entering the hall, I spot my closest friends and without saying anything, we go and sit together. I think that we do it instinctively because if we get bored we can always chat or pass around a note to while away the time (not text each other, as mobiles are banned during the school day).

As I observe my classmates, I know how heavy-going weekdays are like when you are 17. We all look tired, and although it's been quiet to some extent because there have been several Guidance talks, we are all preparing for the forthcoming exams. There's quite a lot at stake and I can safely say that the majority of the class, like me, are going to spend whatever time there's left in the month to study right up to the last minute.

We are all seated. I leave my bag with my books at my feet and take out a folder to lean on with a couple of sheets of paper, which they told us to bring to this talk.

The Assembly Hall has always felt like a place for fun events. We've come for Christmas and end-of-year celebrations, as well as others organised by the school. The first school assembly of the school year is here and this is when the Head Teacher informs us very seriously about what to expect, new changes from last year and above all, rules that we need to follow during the year. That is perhaps the most serious moment that I've experienced in this hall, with the exception, of course, of what's happening now.

Everything seems too formal. Dressed in a suit, the speaker giving the talk mounts the stage.

At first, it seems different because no one at the school wears a tie everyday, and when I see someone so well dressed, I feel somewhat put off because I wonder if he's put on a suit and tie merely to talk to us, or if he wants to demonstrate something that will make no sense.

He's a man of swarthy complexion, of average height, wearing a blue pinstriped suit, a light blue shirt and a dark tie with tiny designs which I can't make out from where I'm sitting.

I recall a conversation at home among the adults who were saying that, depending on what you wanted to achieve, when you stood up to speak in public you had to wear a tie of one colour or another. I recognise that, following this principle, I can't work out beforehand what this man is about. Standing at the edge of the stage, he's making his way slowly from one side to the other as if waiting for the opportune silence to begin speaking.

From his appearance, I guess that he's in his forties. He seems deep in thought as he walks. Could he be nervous before he speaks in public? They've prepared a small table on one side of the stage, where he puts his laptop he uses to present the slides that he's going to use.

I see a glass of water on the table. It's half full. I don't see any bottle to pour out more water. It's strange, but perhaps he thinks that half a glass of water is sufficient for his talk... I look to one side and see that the teacher organizing the Orientation week, goes up three stairs onto the stage. He approaches the microphone.

The hall is large, two floors high, and the stage is a metre above ground level, the height of the seats in the front row. Two large beige curtains, drawn to the sides, frame the area which the person moving across the stage will be able to use.

There's a projector which, like the cinema, projects images on the speaker's laptop onto the large white screen to support his explanation. In fact, we're already watching the first image.

I suppose that the speaker has changed the black image which we saw at the beginning for the first transparency to grab our attention.

There's silence among us. There are sixty of us students and no one's sitting in the first three rows in the hall. I think that we all believed that if we sat there, chances are that we would be picked if the speaker wanted any volunteers. Not so voluntary, in that case!

There seems to be some silent communication between the speaker and our teacher about the lights in the hall. Finally, from the signals they're making, they're going to leave the lights on all the time. It's just as well. I'm thankful because if they switch off the lights around our seats, with it being the last period on a Friday, I don't know how many of us will be able to guarantee that we won't end up shutting our eyes. Not I, of course.

"Good morning," begins the teacher, speaking into the microphone he had taken, while I observe that the speaker, looking at him, has stopped pacing at the edge of the stage. "We are going to start the final session of these Orientation days on your future as students and as workers."

By this time, I can assure you that none of us is looking at him. All of us, and I looked around at my companions to check, are reading the slide that the speaker has put up on the screen. On a white background, he puts up a title:

7-17
THE EXPERIENCE

Preparing for your development
as a student and as a worker

Glen Lapson

At least it looks like it's not going to be the usual talk in which a professional tells you all about the benefits of what he studied and his work, and tries to convince you that you have to study. The teacher is talking now. He must have said the name of the speaker, but I wasn't paying attention.

"The person who is going to talk to you for the next few hours is a past student of this school. He completed his university studies in Industrial Engineering, and afterwards, worked at several corporations. At age 37, he went back to study and did his MA in Business Administration. In addition to being a friend, he is a good person."

This last statement makes me turn to look at the teacher and, on reflex, I look at the speaker who, in his suit and tie, is calmly looking at him. A good person! This is something I have not heard lately. They always talk about a great professional or distinguished person, but to talk about a *good person*? ... I think that this is the first time

16

I've heard it in a presentation. I wonder, was it necessary to say it? At least, he succeeded in grabbing my interest in it.

"Today, he is going to talk about his experience, to share it with you."

The teacher stops talking and looks at the speaker. Then, he quietly goes down the stairs to sit in the second row and to focus his attention on the stage. We sit still, quietly, just waiting while we take in the image.

"Good morning and thank you for your introduction," he addresses the teacher who has just sat down. It's obvious that they've known each other for a long time, and from their glances, there's a lot of affection for each other. He starts speaking in a low voice, as he walks quietly from one side of the stage to the other. Looking at all of us, he continues, "I too was over there exactly 30 years ago." He points to the seats in the hall where we're sitting, "and I can tell you that I am proud to be here with you today."

I don't know quite what to make of this. I came prepared for just another talk. I sat down with everyone and supposed no one expected anything different from what we had been told so far. Suddenly, I observe the speaker, with great agility, moving quickly towards the computer to change to the next slide. I watch it and I have to admit that it completely grabs our attention.

CHAPTER 2

The colour and the smell have changed since the last time I was here, but the feeling continues to be the same: a mixture of nervousness, joy and pride. I have always wondered if this last feeling, before speaking in public, is the line between vanity and the desire to be the center of attention. Then you forget all the distractions and try to do the best you can. The main issue is that the 'best I can' will not be what I think or do, but rather what others who come to listen to me think at the end. So I must put myself in their shoes.

I have mounted this stage many times and the mixture of emotions continues to be the same. I remember the first time was when I was a couple of years younger than the young people who are looking up at me now.

It was for Christmas that year. They asked us to participate and put on a performance at the school. At that time, I got on well with a group of school mates and we put on small sketches ranging from comedy to the Theatre of the Absurd. I cannot say if we were better in the rehearsals or on the day when we performed in front of the school. We must have done it well because at least no-one whistled at the end, and someone in the corridor told us afterwards that he had liked it.

The truth is that whenever we had an opportunity to play a role or put on a performance, several of us put our names down. At first, the fear of being ridiculed was enormous, but gradually it disappeared.

I remember with affection our last performance when, in our last year of high school, we put on *Waiting for Godot*, written at the end of the 1940s by Samuel Beckett.

Over the years, I have read this work again several times, and each time I discover new meanings. Indeed, I do not know if I really understood what the writer was trying to say the first time I read it. Today, without realising it, I have come to talk about something that is linked to it.

I have decided to make a start. I am aware that if you have to prepare a talk for 17-year-olds, last thing on a Friday afternoon, it is better to start with something different or you are doomed to total failure, with heads drooping in their seats, yawning and even some eyes closed.

I remember the precise moment when we prepared the session a month ago with the teachers who were coordinating the Orientation days for young people. We agreed on the ideas that I was going to try to get across and I was all too aware that I would have to think carefully about how to present them. I liked the ideas that emerged and how the main thread of the talk would be developed. What overwhelmed me was the sheer challenge of addressing such a demanding audience as the one I have before me today.

When you speak in public, however interesting the message you want to convey may appear, you can fail completely if you do not express it appropriately. I knew what I wanted to say and I chose this first slide to try to connect with the audience.

At last I have started. I am nervous. I can feel them looking at me although I cannot glean their feelings, whether they are negative or positive about my being here. I want to be close to them in the format and language I use, but there is a 30-year gap between us, and depending on the role that I play, I can make an absolute fool of myself.

It is not the first time that I have spoken in public. On previous occasions, my nervousness has left me before my talk has started. But today is different. I am doing it before a future generation. I am doing it before myself and my school mates 30 years aback. I am going to do it.

I turn towards them after putting on the second slide. I stay silent, looking at them from the edge of the stage.

"When I was around your age, I bought a book." I pause and let them watch me. "Back then, we liked doing leisure activities and we were planning to become summer camp leaders for small children. So, when I saw a book which could help me to put on activities with my school mates, to prepare plans for the future with other children or young people, I tried to buy it. Or, a less expensive option, considering my personal finance, was for a family member or friend to give it to me for my next birthday.

That book was called _Posters con Humor (Posters with Humour)_, written by Herminio Otero in 1982. It had a great impact on me. It was a book of activities based on posters drawn by various people, and it was the first book I had ever owned and I would then use it for many years.

The title of Chapter 6 of the book was _De la Huida al Compromiso_ [1] _(From Flight to Commitment)_, illustrated by a 1982 drawing by Quino. I suppose it was fate. I found myself standing in a shop and the first page I opened the book on was this one.

And I saw the drawing. On a vertical sheet of paper, with the upper two-thirds of the page completely blank, my gaze was directed to the lower one-third where there was the drawing. On it, the author had presented a very powerful message with very few illustrations. Working together afterwards on exercises suggested in the book, the meaning that we extracted was always the same: faced with the problems of the world, many people were running away from it to avoid the obligation of finding solutions for the problem.

Quino had succeeded in conveying a powerful idea with a simple drawing, which began to impact on my development as a young person growing up. If I could speak to him some time, the first thing I would do is to thank him for that drawing."

I take a step back and point in silence at the drawing projected on the screen.

"From the outset, it attracted my attention and I then discovered that the great cartoonist, Joaquín Salvador Lavado Tejón Quino who, with so little, expressed so much.

At that time, when we were 17, there was a slogan that someone had painted on the walls: 'Let the world stop, so that I can get off'. There was quite a lot of disillusionment in society, caused mainly by the economic crisis in the country. This culture of running away had begun to spread to some young people.

It has had a significant effect on me because I have remembered this drawing many times throughout my life. Indeed, from time to time I think of it when I am faced with specific complicated situations in life, in which I really wanted to escape and run away."

I stop talking. I go up to the computer and put on the second slide with the drawing:

SLIDE 2

I remain in silence and watch their faces. I wonder if I had captured their attention. I hope so.

"This is the reason for drawing it again, but differently." I point to the drawing projected on the screen. "I understand that this is the only way that a 17-year-old can confront what he is going to experience.

Today I have not come simply to give a talk. The intention is for us to live the experience together. An experience that allows us to present enough reasons to those little people in the drawing who have decided to enter the world and not run away, to do something important, to make a contribution to improve and change it. Because that is what it is all about: our education, which is on-going, has to have as its final objective: to enable us to improve and to change.

I obviously assume that we can all have the utopian dream of building a new world in which there is no poverty and where there is a stable peace. It is a great objective that we should have as citizens in a continuously developing world. Over time, we will realize that we should set short-term objectives in order to achieve those other overall objectives.

Therefore, today we are going to present some suggestions. On one hand, to discover what our first objective in the job we have is, and on the other, how we can develop to achieve it and be sure that we are taking the path that we have set."

I approach the table and take two blank sheets of paper.

"For today's session, you have brought two blank sheets of paper." I hold up the ones I have. "One of them is for an activity we will do later. And the other, I suggest you fold it in half." I give them a moment to do it. "On the right-hand side, I would like you to note down the good ideas from the experience we are going to have today. On the left, note down the titles of the books that I am going to mention.

What I am going to share with you are real experiences that I have had, as well as those of my family, friends and work colleagues; an experience that was beyond me was a role that, when I was your age, I could not even begin to imagine: the role of a parent. Someday, perhaps, you may also have to perform this role.

In addition, I will share with you books that I have read, and how I have applied them to real life situations because, in my life, books have always played a very important role."

CHAPTER 3

I've to admit that he's succeeded in getting me to listen to him. My classmates next to me are also listening. Of course there's a difference between giving a talk and sharing an experience. I only hope that it's true and that he's not playing with us by using dialectics.

The explanation of the Quino drawing and the adapted drawing were a good start. I had seen some Mafalda drawings in some of my parents' old books, in which the author was able to get across many concepts with just a few drawings. The one with people running away from the world, compared to the group of young people carrying tools entering it, shows a great contrast that is very expressive.

The advantage of having two older sisters, so different from each other, gives you an insight into those two possibilities shown on the screen. I believe that I can put my older sister in the group running away and my middle sister in the one facing reality.

Let's see how this man continues the 'experience', as he calls it, because I think that I'm going to see my family reflected here.

He has just changed the slide and now there's only a definition.

According to Wikipedia:

"In a large part of the world,
the age at which an individual is
considered to be fully capable,
is normally understood to be
between 16 and 22 years old."

Glen Lapson

I see that he's waiting until we finish reading it in order to continue his explanation.

"This means that, at 16, you begin to have a set of rights and new responsibilities." He regards us in silence for a moment and then continues, "Usually, we talk about 18. The majority of 17-year-old students would agree that the pressure exerted by family, education and society itself supersedes the challenge posed by university or work. 17 is usually considered the age of 'one year from 18', when we change as a person, have more rights, more responsibilities.

It is the moment when we consider plans for the future, pose questions and, above all, feel curious about what is to come afterwards. But it does not stop there. With the passage of time, we plan again and again, ask ourselves questions and, even though some may lose it, we should maintain a curiosity for the future.

The top *tip* from this experience (and perhaps I may write about it sometime in a book) is for those who are 17 today, and for those who were 17, to ask the same question again, at least every ten years, when you are 27, 37 and 47, ... And for everyone who has at some point planned to run away as in the first Quino drawing that I have described, but has always wanted to be in the second group.

It does not matter what decision you make in the coming years, whether to continue studying or join the world of work. For either option, I have the same tips."

I wonder if my sisters attended a similar talk when they were my age. I wonder how two educated people with the same family background could be so different. I ought to tell them what this man is saying: that every 10 years they should review whether they are doing what they want or ought to be doing. What is certain is that when they give me advice, they speak to me from different worlds... or perhaps from different views of the world.

I see the speaker staring into the distance as if trying to recall the past. Without checking to see if we are looking at him or not, he begins to talk again.

"I am going to share a personal experience:

Experience 1: Meeting of young people
On 19 March 1983, five 16 and 17-year-olds had gone for a trek across the mountains, some 100 km from this city. It was 3 in the morning of the second night of the outing. They were talking, huddled in their sleeping bags

---

27

in a tent. They had been walking for two days on trails linking several villages in the chosen area. The whole activity was part of a training program.

Their experience was unique because they did not know each other well before they undertook the walk, but by the end, they had become very close. The main problem was the snow which they had not expected and everything that happened afterwards.

But what was important was that on that second night, when they could not sleep because of the cold, they were talking about what they might do when they were older. Such was their closeness that it led them to talk about their future in private. They all had many dreams and projects that they wanted to achieve. One saw himself as an entrepreneur, another in the army, and another to own a hairdresser's salon, while the others had no concrete plans. So, they simply shared their hopes for the future.

In the end, and in the middle of a difficult and pressurised situation, which they would all finally overcome, they made a decision: to meet up in 17 years time to see how life had turned out for each of them. On 1 January 2000, they were all going to meet up at an agreed place in the center of the city where they lived.

30 years on, I still remember that moment. It was unique for me because we had shared a very special experience, but I will never forget when we five arrived at the train station in the last village. We were tired and quite filthy after three days of walking, carrying our backpacks and tents, but proud of what we had done, united and, above all, ready to catch the train which we saw coming from the mountains, just at that moment, and was about to stop at the station where we were waiting. Since then, whenever I hear the metaphor (and I use it often) of catching the train that passes through your life, I always remember that moment.

However, I have to confess that I did not attend the meeting 17 years later.

I often think about it and I wonder if anyone went. I wonder what sort of lives they would have had. After a few years, we lost contact with each other because of circumstances in life, although I have been able to follow the lives of some of them through casual meetings with mutual acquaintances. I know some of them are OK, although I do not have information about all of them. One of them married a university colleague and when we met casually years later, I remember the joy on our faces when we saw each other. But when we met, we did not ask if either of us had gone to that meeting 17 years later.

I have often thought about that key experience over the years, mainly when I was working as a volunteer with 17-year-olds on leisure time activities. I thought about it when I was studying and often during my working life. I thought about it again this morning when I arrived at the school for this session. Knowing that there is always a train arriving, if we are at the station where it is passing, we have the option of either getting on or not getting on.

I did not attend the meeting. But I have never stopped thinking about the dreams we had and how full of life we were at 16 and 17 years of age. That reflection made me review all my life's experiences since then. Everything *that I will share with you today springs from this recollection. I consider myself fortunate for all the experiences I have had; I consider myself fortunate for having lived each minute of my life, sometimes alone and at other times with others, because I have to confess that today at 47, I have at least as many or perhaps even more dreams than I had when I was 17, so many more desires to live the life that awaits me.*

"This is precisely the aim of today's experience. Whatever the reason for your being here, what is clear is that, throughout your life, trains have passed, are passing and will pass. What is important are the attitudes and abilities you have and have developed, those that will influence whether you take the train, what you do on that train, if you get off afterwards or even look for other trains to catch.

Often, we have to be aware of our current situation; we have to be aware whether a train is really going to pass, or if we are on the wrong track."

He stops speaking and goes back to his computer. He turns, looks at us in silence as if he thought that we weren't watching him, and presses the button on the mouse, moving on to the next slide: [2]

SLIDE 4

Herminio Otero (1982)
Posters con humor. Editorial C.C.S.

CHAPTER 4

I hope that they have the same feeling I had when I saw this drawing for the first time in the book *Posters con Humor,* with the young man waiting at the station. With each year that passes, we realize that many people are in a state of futile waiting. I always want to shout at the young man in the drawing, "IT'S NOT GOING TO COME!"

"IT'S NOT GOING TO COME", I would also have to say to many people who do nothing to effect change, but wait and wait for something to change without doing anything. When there are problems, many of them look to throw the blame on others around them and to justify their 'bad luck'. Obviously, at times it does not depend on us, but we have to acknowledge the other times when it does and we are passive.

Now, I do not see any bored faces, so I try to use even plainer language to continue to hold their attention.

"Son, now that you are 17, the most important thing you have to do is to study." I continue, "How many of us have heard this speech? And above all, those of us who have children, how many of us have repeated it? Or even, how many of those who have children are thinking of saying it?

This statement is absolutely right. A young person of 17, with the resources and conditions, has to study, and not only to study to pass exams, but also to study in order to learn.

Many times, at this age, they do not know the *why* or the *what for*. For this, we rely on parents and teachers to know the answer. Perhaps, the only thing you can see in front of a person when he is studying is books. Sometimes, you can only see the text of the subject he is studying. Sometimes, it is the reality that is missing. The 'bridge' between what he is studying and life itself is not there.

It is clear that the 'baseline' for a 17-year-old is to study as much as possible in order to learn. What is also clear is that he needs to see and understand the *usefulness* (a word I will come back to later on) of what is being studied.

Those who had helped their fathers or mothers at home with electrical repairs, or even those who, on their own initiative, had had experience with electricity or electronics as a hobby, they were the students who asked the most interesting questions in a physics class, not only to learn about the subject, but also to put into practice what they have learnt.

Those who had practised music by learning to play an instrument, or simply the theory of music, had a greater talent for mathematics, and have increased their insight and ability for abstract reasoning.

And of course those who, at 17, were active and intensely interested in sport, tended to be much more interested in biology. In some cases, they introduced topics that they had studied in anatomy, and in others they needed to understand how injuries had occurred or they could deal with those they knew about.

That is, study yes and a lot, and even more importantly, look for parallels in life."

I approach the computer and put on the next slide:

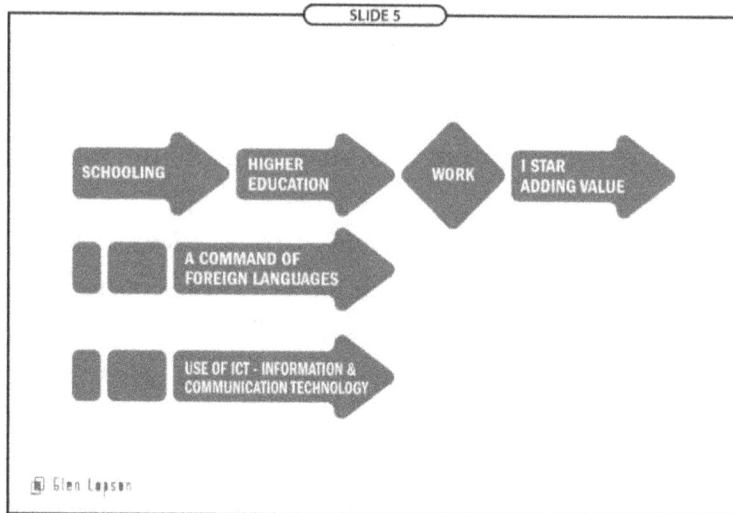

I wait a couple of seconds, and then go to the front of the stage to get closer to them.

"At 17, you think about what happens afterwards. If we often see our choices reduced to just two, studying or working, let us not forget that there is a third, which is a combination of the two. Whatever choice you make, it is important to start by drawing up a plan.

When we were 17 and we were presented with this choice, we would look at those who had passed through this phase, had even completed the training process and joined the labour market.

The drawing, which you have in front of you, represents the development that my generation experienced. When we analyzed previous generations, i.e. those who at that time were 10, 20 or 30 years older, we would see that they had moved in a trajectory from studies that I like (university or otherwise) to finding a job that I like.

The economic situation has changed, and in our generation, the paradigm was different: when we joined the labour market, they were demanding studies, languages and a command of ICT (Information and Communication Technology).

This is where problems began, because the situation gradually made the labour market more competitive. Some did not find work in the field they had studied. Some accepted change and prepared for it, others continued waiting like the young man above on the discontinued track.

I have often felt like a witness to my own period. I like observing, not for mere curiosity, but to see what may be of benefit for the future from what is happening in the present or has happened in the past. Indeed, while I was studying at university and observed those who were finishing, it was already evident that the model above was beginning to fail. I have memories of many people, most of all, of those who saw the change in time and began to adapt.

When those of my generation and later years tried to access the labour market, conditions made many people feel frustrated because they felt that they had done all that they had been asked to, but still could not find their dream job, the job that they had been promised in the beginning. THEY HAD DONE ALL THAT THEY WERE REQUIRED TO DO, BUT SOCIETY WAS NOT GIVING THEM WHAT THEY DEMANDED FROM IT.

It seemed that Society was to blame. This continues to be the case.

Some people become frustrated, others learn and adapt, and there are many who complain and demand that Society gives them work.

In this learning experience, many have seen that the paradigm has changed. Now the demand is no longer on Society. The vast majority have decided to stop blaming Society and have started to take action. The demand is on the individual himself because it is Society that demands it. The new model requires studies, foreign languages, ICT and... '*Something more*'.

And this is a fact. When my generation went out into the labour market after completing their university studies, we were already asking ourselves questions about this '*something more*'. Over the years, it has become a requirement. In a job interview, when candidates are asked what they can bring to the company in addition to their studies, it is important that they are able to give an answer.

And this is the answer that I bring to you today: START TRAINING AT 17, NEVER STOP TRAINING AND REVIEW IT EVERY 10 YEARS."

Experience 2: Personal Interview: the Mountain

I remember that, at one of my job interviews, at a particular point in the meeting, the manager interviewing me asked me about my hobbies. At that time, I practised rock climbing and mountaineering with quite a lot more intensity than I do currently, always as an enthusiast,

---

never performing great feats, but always trying to do a little more each time I went. I have always enjoyed it and continue to do so.

My response was quite modest, but I must have answered with such confidence that her second question, still in a very light tone, was to ask me what was the last mountain I had climbed. I answered her still very quietly, mentioning one of the mountains of over three thousand meters that I had climbed in the Pyrenees at the time. Looking at me this time directly in the eye and more seriously, she asked me about the route of ascent that I had used. I understood that her questions and my answers were a clear strategy to get to know me and to analyze if this 'something more' was real and had value.

When the interview was over, I left quietly as I remembered how my response to that lady meant that she herself was much friendlier afterwards. It turned out that she too was a mountaineer and when she spoke, she did so with passion. For the rest of the interview, we only talked about mountaineering, but not of mountains. We talked about how to organize departures, excursions and routes. What problems generally occur with climbing/mountaineering companions, budgets, the resources that were needed and the most suitable strategies for going up the mountain.

She had assessed my abilities through my hobby.

"To sum up the theme of my talk with you today, I am trying to bring my own experience and that of my closest friends when we attended job interviews, as well as my own experience in recruiting staff both for work in voluntary organizations, and in multinational companies as part of my main job.

At all interviews, candidates try to sell themselves (as we all do when it is our turn). Each person tries to sell the best of himself. Since they are always competitive processes, you have to try to stand out from the other candidates. To stand out in this way, it is often this '*something more*' that can make all the difference.

But, what is this '*something more*' that they are looking for?"

I stop and wait silently, trying to arouse their curiosity. Now here comes the most important part of the message. I have to get it right in order to give it the importance that it deserves. If I describe it all from a theoretical point-of-view, I do not think I will achieve my aim. I must give concrete examples, and I am giving them. I hope I do not give too many. I do not want them to think that I have come just to talk about myself. I have been to talks in which the speaker has overstated his own achievements, and by the end I had put on an impervious barrier against everything he had said afterwards. I put these thoughts to one side and change the slide.

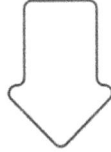

ADD
VALUE!

Glen Lopson

I allow them a second to read it and, in an enthusiastic tone, and going even closer to them with my hands raised, I say:

"THIS IS THE KEY: ADD VALUE!

THIS IS ONE OF THE PROPOSALS I BRING TO YOU TODAY: WE MUST ADD VALUE!

It is true that the idea is common to all sectors and organizations. What they are looking for is: what will this person be able to do to ADD VALUE to the company, organization, association or group that he intends to join? Even if the organization does not value the concept of ADDING VALUE in the selection process (as it can happen in jobs that are accessed merely by written test or exam), throughout his future career trajectory, the individual will be assessed by this criterion."

CHAPTER 5

On this last point, I think that he's gone over the top in his anecdotes. Although if they are real as he says, they help to explain what he's trying to say. "Add Value?" I've heard this phrase several times, and I've always associated it with the world of business, especially when it comes to material goods, but never had I thought it applied to people like us. He's now changing the slide:

SLIDE 7

Now it is time to prepare how you will respond when this moment comes.

And what if this moment is within the next two years because you have to go out to work for personal/family reasons? And what if it is now?

What are you going to add that is different?

What value are you going to bring?

Glen Lopson

He's just added an important slant to the talk.

He must have read my thoughts because, just then, he walks to the left-hand side of the stage and, bending forward slightly, he begins to talk again in a soft voice.

"Here, there are two scenarios: on the one hand, a young person of 17 who has to start thinking about what answer he is going to give when, years later (OR MAYBE TOMORROW), in a job interview, they ask him about this '*something more*'; or if he himself decides to start on his own journey, he will have to know what is this '*something more*' that he will bring to his own company or concept, that is, what can he do to bring *Added Value* to the organization or group. On the other hand, a person of 27, 37, 47, etc.... is often analyzed by the group on his ability to *Add Continuous Value*.

But how do you add value?"

He stops talking and keeps looking at us. Then, he walks from one side of the stage to the other in silence. My friend on the right looks at me and shrugs her shoulders. I do the same. The speaker stops, looks at us and continues.

"It is very easy to answer the question if you are a sporty person. All those who practise a sport, either games sports or mountain climbs, know that on the day of a match or a climb if you turn up without having trained beforehand, you will not be able to perform to the required standard. An important part of the success of a sporting activity lies in the training and in the preparation.

It is the same with 'Adding Value'. If a young person completes university or non-university studies and enters the labour market, and only then starts Adding Value for the first time, it is unlikely that he will get a job, or else it will take a long time before he gets one. Adding Value does not just happen spontaneously. And of course, during the job recruitment process, it will be difficult to demonstrate anything in this area.

Therefore, it seems reasonable to think that if a young person of 17 intends to Add Value professionally within a few years, he should be 'training himself' on how to Add Value now and not put it off.

Now it is time to prepare how you will respond when the moment comes.

And what if that moment is the next two years because you have to go out to work for personal/family reasons? And what if it is now?

What are you going to add, that is new?

What value are you going to bring?

How are you going to train yourself to add value?"

He approaches the computer and changes the slide.

SLIDE 8

HOW TO ADD **VALUE?**

BY EDUCATION

BY TRAINING MYSELF TO ADD VALUE FROM NOW

Glen Lapson

"It is very clear that training, at least at this age and in subsequent years, is the main source of knowledge and experience for Adding Value in the future. In other words, studying is very important. One has to make every effort not only to pass exams, but also to understand and to learn. Of course, it will be easier if you study by applying what you have learnt to real issues, let's say, in the present, past and future."

__Experience 3: Tents__

I remember that, at the start of my university studies, I worked as a volunteer in a leisure activities team, organizing free time activities for children and young people. In those days, one of our problems was the excessive time it took to do small and large-scale repairs to tents for the outings we had to manage. It was a significant number of tents, but the greatest variable was the repair that had to be done over the year for them to be ready to be used when they were needed. So, we had to draw up long lists on paper which kept changing and being binned in the end.

At that time, two of the instructors were studying computer programming, and it was then that it occurred to them to use database programs to manage this task. It turned out to be very good idea for a small group such as ours. It was something that allowed us to save a lot of time and money.

It is difficult to imagine now, given that anyone can create a database with the multiple applications available today, but in 1986 it was extraordinary. The lesson of that experience was that it was possible to apply what we were studying to what we were doing in our spare time, and of course, it was a great incentive to continue learning 'useful things'.

It's difficult to imagine because it's so easy with the programs we use today. Perhaps someone has created an APP to solve such a problem. I get the idea, but I fail to see its relevance. I suppose that, as he says, it was difficult in those days.

I have got distracted and missed part of what he is saying. I pay attention once more:

"...you will bring the knowledge and skills from the education you have received, according to the studies you do.

Training in Adding Value is the second element that every young person should always keep in mind in preparing for the future.

Everything that you start doing today can continue to grow. You may know people who help you to add value and those to whom you can add value - people you have helped and those with whom you have done business or shared activities. Basically, this idea gives value and, furthermore at a professional level, it can reinforce your development and that of your group.

CONCLUSION:
TRAIN YOURSELF TO ADD VALUE."

CHAPTER 6

It is the most important concept that I have introduced today, and I hope I have attracted their attention because, next, I have to link it to the second part of the session. What I have to do now is to make sure that they do not misinterpret the concept of Adding Value. Someone might think that it is an absolutely utilitarian vision of people, and that if a person does not add value, he has no social worth. That is absolutely **not** what I want to convey. So I have to present suitable arguments quickly.

I head to the far end of the stage, lower the tone of my voice and hope that they look at me. Then I continue:

"So, what is this concept of Adding Value? And more importantly, where can I Add Value today?

When we talk of Adding Value, we must take into account that we are referring both to abilities that we have been acquiring via our training and to activities we are carrying out at the same time, but above all, to attitudes: how we behave is not only what others see in us, but also what we succeed in getting others to value in us, because we contribute towards achieving something positive in the group in which we find ourselves.

We have seen colleagues who participate in school activities, sports, culture and music, in NGOs, youth associations, politics, in jobs that allow you to maintain the level of study and even in their own families. There are young people who, at 17, add value to their own families, maintaining happiness, helping in everyday chores, proposing and organizing family activities, and even taking care of sick and elderly family members."

Experience 4: Young person with a commitment at home

I shall never forget a classmate whose mother was sick. Her mother was unable to do things for herself and needed them to do everything for her. My friend was the fourth of five siblings, and because of the way the family was organized, I remember that by the time we saw her first thing in the morning, she had already been up for several hours, helping at home because before she went to school she had to have everything ready for her mom. "I had to organize myself and make time," she told me a few days ago.

Her mother continued in that condition for many years, as my friend told me years later when we met on the street. In fact, when she was at university, there were times that demanded greater effort of her and that also involved robbing her of hours of sleep in the morning before beginning her day at university.

"It's obvious that if finance for my education is not guaranteed, the first thing we have to do is to make sure that it is there. There are many people for whom study is not their sole major activity; instead, it has to be supplemented by paid employment."

I go to the computer and change the slide.

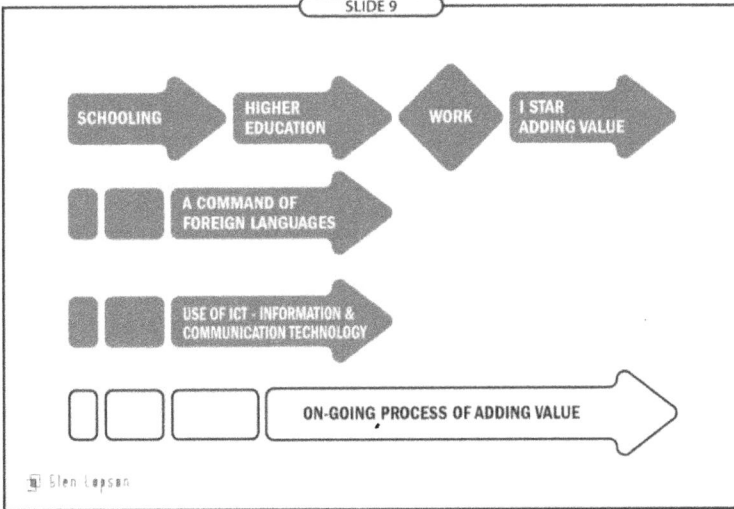

The moment has arrived. I am aware that now is an important turning point for the session. I have to do it well; I have to present it in an appropriate manner. I have decided to use my own experience because I have been involved for many years with groups and organizations where I have learnt a lot and now it is the moment to talk about it.

"How to Add Value? How do I train myself to add value?

The proposal I bring before you today is how to oversee your development in **7 AREAS OF GROWTH.**

A long time ago, I referred to them as the 7 areas of personal development, but I prefer to call them fields or areas in which I have to grow. These areas are influenced by what happens in the environment; they have to be tended; where I can bring in harvest, and above all, after gathering the harvest, to distribute, share or 'sell'.

Whenever I do interviews in the recruitment selection process, I try to see the person within each of these areas. Everyone may have his own technique and today I am sharing mine with you. Above all, they are areas that we consciously or unconsciously work day-by-day, and in our relationships within voluntary or business organizations, we relate with others who also work the same areas.

If you create a group or join an existing one, and want to undertake a project that projects into the future, I recommend that you consider yourself and others within these **7 AREAS OF GROWTH."**

I go up to the computer again and change the transparency.

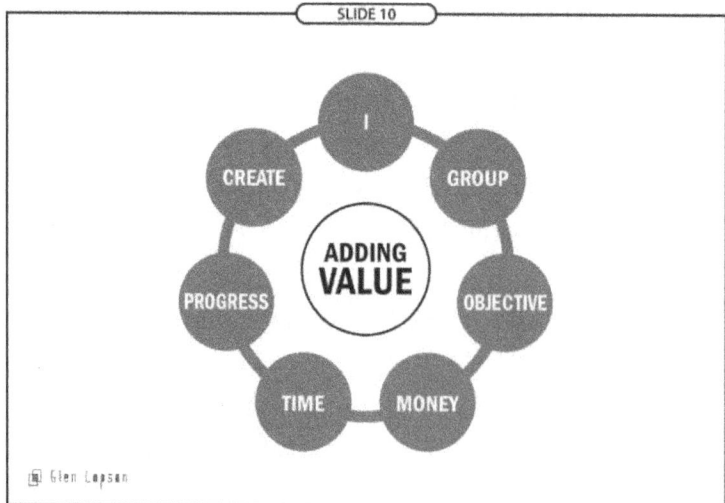

SLIDE 10

CREATE
GROUP
ADDING VALUE
OBJECTIVE
PROGRESS
MONEY
TIME

Glen Lapson

"And this was the second secret that I wanted to reveal today. First, we have spoken about the need to Add Value and to train ourselves from the age of 17; now we discover that there are **SEVEN AREAS OF GROWTH** to consider in our development. But before continuing the presentation, we are going to do something different. You have all brought a blank sheet of paper. I am going to ask you to put it in front of you and take a pen. We are going to do a special exercise."

Standing at the edge of the stage, I show them the sheet of paper in vertical orientation.

"First, put the page in a vertical position and draw a line horizontally from side to side to divide it into two equal parts. The exercise has two parts. In the first, I am going to give you ten seconds to make as many dots as you can with your pens in the top half."

I give them a moment in silence, and then continue:

"If you are all ready, let's start... Start now!"

I count down ten seconds. Everyone begins very quickly to make dots with their pens in the top half of the sheet. When they finish, I shout:

"Stop! Put down your pens."

I allow them to look at each other, to keep them curious about the objective of the exercise, and to see if everyone has done the same.

I wait for them to quiet down and look at me.

"Now, count how many dots you have made. Note down the number of dots that you have made on the upper right hand side in the top half of the page and encircle it."

Again, I give them time to do it, and when I see that most of them are waiting quietly, I continue:

"Very well. Here is the second part of the exercise."

I become more serious and raise my voice to give the instructions for this second part.

"Now I am going to give you the same amount of time as before, ten seconds, and you have to estimate how many dots you would make if...". At this point, I raise my voice even louder, almost shouting. "...YOU DID IT AS FAST AS YOU COULD, AS IF YOU HAD MAXIMUM PRESSURE TO DO IT AND SOMEONE WAS SHOUTING AND ARGUING THAT YOU ARE NOT DOING IT FASTER THAN THE OTHERS.

I stop speaking for a moment. I observe that they have become serious by the attitude that I have taken, and lowering my voice, while I remain standing at the edge of the stage, I continue speaking in a much lower voice.

"Please note down the estimated number of dots on the upper right hand side of the bottom half of the page and encircle it."

The students are working in silence to do their own calculations and to note down the number. They do not look at each other, but work individually. When I see that almost all have finished and are looking at me, I continue.

"Perfect. Are you ready?"

I hear a general 'yes'. I observe that they are all eager to challenge themselves. With pens ready in one hand, they look eagerly at the second half of the page which is at present blank.

"START!"

I again give them ten seconds. I hear the insistent movement of all the pens, impacting quickly on the pages of the young people who now remind me of what I was doing 30 years before. At the end, I shout:

"STOP! You may put down your pens. You know what to do now."

I watch them counting the dots they had made on the bottom half of the page in silence, without answering me, and without the need for me to say anything more to them.

"Now, note down the number of dots you have made in the lower right hand side of the bottom half of the page you used to make the dots. When you have finished, talk to the people around you about what you have done."

CHAPTER 7

This looks like one of those tasks they sometimes do with us in a session. I haven't come across it before and it seems very interesting. When he tells us to make dots on the sheet, it seems a little ridiculous, but my friends and I look at each other, shrug our shoulders and smile as if we have nothing to lose; asked to make a fool of ourselves, we'd do it all together so, it will be less noticeable.

After we have finished, it is obvious that the speaker is going try to sum up and draw some lesson from the activity. He is looking at us and waiting for us to be quiet. Since he started this activity, I have been wondering what he is trying to do with it. I keep asking myself the same question. I don't like doing things without clearly understanding their purpose or at least being able to guess or work out what the objective is.

When he told us a second time that he was going to give us the same amount of time to put dots on the lower part, I thought that I could guess the reason for all this. I have done what I thought I was supposed to, but now that I have seen what my companions around me have done, I realise that I have done something different.

"Are you with me?"

The speaker's words shake me out of my reverie and bring me back to the exercise. Let's see how he continues because I think that I have done it badly. Will I be the only one who has done this?

"In the first place", the speaker continues, "I appreciate the interest you have shown in the exercise that I have given you. You have taken it very seriously and I assure you that it is much appreciated. I have no doubt that you are a group that takes everything you do seriously."

He pauses, returns to the back of the stage, takes the chair that they had left him, brings it to the front of the stage to be closer to us and then sits down looking at us with a slight smile.

"You have all counted the dots you made in the top half of your sheet. Then, you have estimated the amount you were going to make in the bottom half. Now I have a question - how many of you have a similar number in the bottom half as your estimate?"

We all look at each other and begin raising our hands. I count the number of hands that are raised and it seems that only half of us have done practically the same amount as we had estimated we were going to do.

"Seeing the hands that are raised", the speaker continues, "another question arises: the rest of you, have you done more or less than you estimated?"

Almost all of those who had not raised their hands immediately call out:

"Less!"

"More!"

That leads to some laughter among us, but we immediately grow quiet to listen to him.

The man remains seated while he looks at us, smiling slightly as before.

"It's interesting. Each of you will have to assess yourselves."

He is quiet for a moment for us to joke about the comment, and then he continues speaking:

"But I am interested in talking about something else. How many of you have estimated that you were going to do fewer dots than you have done in the top half?"

Nobody answers. Me neither.

"Well, that is good. And now another question. How many of you have estimated many more dots than you did in the top half?"

There is some murmuring, laughter and many hands go up. Not mine. My position is camouflaged by the group.

"Why did you estimate more dots?"

There is a short silence and gradually, my companions begin to call out loudly the same comments:

"Because you told us that we had to do it as fast as we could and do as many as we can!"

"Because you shouted at us!"

"Because we can always do better!"

I'm beginning to feel nervous. This could get complicated for me in front of my colleagues if he poses the question which I think that he is going to ask now. It's possible that I'll make an even bigger fool of myself, or quite the reverse, but what is not possible is for nothing to happen. And just at that moment, what I didn't want to happen does.

"How many of you estimated the same number of dots as you had done in the top half?" The speaker stops speaking and looks at us.

I was hoping to avoid this, and I don't know what to do. I am a shy person and I think that I don't deserve what is happening. I look back at the rows behind and no hands go up... and neither in the rows in front. I am not ready for this. I don't want to do it. I observe that my companion to my right has noticed my scores and is looking at me. There's nothing else for it. I have to do it. I finally raise my hand.

The speaker looks at me, while he checks to see if there are other hands up. When at last he sees that there is only me, he looks at me fixedly.

"Could you tell us why?"

I can't open my mouth; I am dying of shame. I don't know if it is better to speak first straight away or...

"Well..." I begin. "I put the same number of points because the first time, I had already reached the limit of my ability, when you said that we had to do it as fast as we could."

The speaker looks at me seriously. There is a moment of tension in the Hall because everyone is silent. How embarrassing to have to speak in front of my companions since I have done something different from the rest of them.

Silence continues in the Hall. The speaker stands up from his chair and looks at me. Suddenly, his face lights up incredibly as he breaks into a broad smile.

"It's unbelievable", he begins as he moves nervously around the stage. "I have done this exercise many times with young people, and even with work teams made up of people in their 30s, engineers and graduates..." He is quiet for moment and then he continues, "… and never has this happened before."

Now, I don't know where to put myself. I have been left exposed in front of all my fellow students, although his smile is preparing me for what is coming.

"There is no single answer for the conclusions of this exercise", he continues. "I will tell you a story and you can tell me what you think."

There is total silence in the Hall. The speaker approaches the edge of the stage, I suppose, for us to pay greater attention.

Experience 5: Recruitment process - points

In December 1985, six young people between 18 and 19 years of age attended recruitment tests for an administrative post in a bank. The tests consisted of some psychometric tests and this exercise.

As they were leaving, the young people shared what they had done in the exercise with each other. Only one of them had put down the same estimate in the second part as he had put down in the top half.

There is absolute quiet. I love how this man controls the silence. We are all listening to him again. I suppose if anyone could see my face, they would think that I look as red as a tomato.

"Do you know who they selected?"

There have been few times in my life that I have ever felt like this. I noticed that my companions are looking at me. But I don't feel embarrassed, but rather a sense of genuine pride. How could I have imagined that a simple exercise in a talk would make me feel like this? This man has succeeded in keeping our attention for the rest of the session because the conclusion of the exercise is heard from mouth to mouth between whispers among the group: "You have to do things well from the very start."

CHAPTER 8

I was not expecting such a surprise. Never before had anyone got it so quickly and so exactly. I think they have noticed how I am feeling. A broad smile has unconsciously escaped me. At first I tried to prevent them from seeing, but it was so obvious that I was surprised, that I think they also deserved to see those feelings they had brought about. After all, what is our human relationship if not to feel and let others feel?

I remember that I did this once with a team of people between the ages of 28 and 35. I had been appointed at a company in another city and it seemed a good way for people to get to know each other and learn about my philosophy on work.

I came prepared to today's session in case the same thing happened again, when one of the people started to debate on the main point of the exercise and that what was important was to be ambitious and always expect to do more than the first time when you had the earlier experience. He was the only person out of a group of eleven who had put double the score in the first half as the estimated figure for the second half. Fortunately, there was little cause for me to intervene as his companions, who knew each other before my arrival, discussed it and all agreed on the main point of the exercise.

As I turn towards the computer to put on the following slide, I notice that the students are excited and they seem to have enjoyed the exercise. For my part, I admit that I like it a lot and it has served me well as a point of departure for the session and that it should not be very long.

"WE START WITH THE FIRST OF THE AREAS OF GROWTH!" I say in a loud voice while I put on the following slide.

SEVEN AREAS OF GROWTH

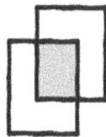

FIRST AREA OF GROWTH: I

"Change your way of looking at things and you will change the things you see."
W. DYER

"If there is something that I regret, it is that which I have not done."
Woody Allen

"The only man who does not make a mistake is the one who NEVER does anything."
Goethe

First area of growth: I

The only way to analyze organizations is to start with the people. We are the foundation of organizations and it is we who make decisions. I am presenting a series of concepts that are important to consider in our development. Some are core principles that emerge from within us, others are more about training, often just as important as other factors in our professional and personal development.

The person 'I' AM

The most important point in this section is to be clear about the person I am: what I am, what I am like, how I develop and, above all, my values, skills and abilities.

Each person has to be aware of their values, assimilate them and make them visible in their own life and daily experiences. Being true to one's own values requires significant effort because our environment seeks to separate us from them, and often we are at odds with even ourselves, going against what we have been taught. It is everyone's decision – a mature decision – to recognise whether we should keep them, increase them or even change them over time.

We all know people who are true weather vanes, changing according to the company they have or the interests of the moment. A person's authenticity, his aims, his fundamental approach and his own sense of purpose in life will all be linked to his day-to-day values and the passage of years.

As a result, it is very important that we have an internal dialogue about what life means to us as soon as possible.

The 'I' who seeks perfection in every act it does

In the same way the exercise with the dots we did before shows how important it is to do things well the first time; it also shows how important it is to look for perfection in what we do.

Experience 6: The Last Samurai

For years, an episode in the film The Last Samurai, *starring Tom Cruise, frequently comes to mind. While living in the mountain village that has received him, the protagonist is amazed most to see that each person in the village seeks perfection in everything he does.* This is highlighted when he says to himself: "...*From the moment they wake they devote themselves to the perfection of whatever they pursue*".

It is a powerful scene that reminds of that necessity, which is perhaps more rooted in oriental philosophies and, therefore, it is something which we must reinforce in the west.

The abstract, transcendental 'I'

Viktor Frankl became famous not for surviving the Nazi concentration camps during the Second World War, nor for all the terrible things he had experienced. Viktor Frankl became famous for writing about how he overcame that experience. His writings are an incredible universal heritage, responsible for launching a new school of psychotherapy: Logotherapy. In his most famous book, *Man's Search for Meaning* (1946), he talks about his experience, adopting a hopeful perspective on the capacity of people to transcend their difficulties and to discover meaning in their lives. He deals with his own sense of purpose in life as a guide on how to find it. Hence, if we analyze the 'I' Area of Growth, we cannot avoid mentioning the implicit transcendence within each of us. It will be different; it will be determined by our beliefs and religious views, or the absence of them. According to Frankl: *"Man alone achieves fulfilment to the extent to which he transcends himself: in the service of a cause or in the love for another."*[3]

I am sure that we will all agree here today that both examples will always lead us to Add Value. Therefore, the person I AM is the first of the areas in our development to Add Value.

This 'I' has nothing to do with self-actualization in itself. Frankl himself tells us: *"By declaring that man is responsible and must actualize the potential meaning of his life, I wish to stress that the true meaning of life is to be discovered in the world rather than within man or his own psyche, as though it were a closed system."* By the same token, the true purpose of human existence cannot be found in what is called 'self-actualization'. *"In other words, self-actualization cannot be achieved as an end in itself, but as a side-effect of self-transcendence."*[4] This message can be understood as the very basis for our Added Value: it is something that we do not do for ourselves, but for others, for the world, from the very transcendence of the individual who does not live alone.

The 'I' who seeks Knowledge and new ideas in all that it does

This suggests that you do not go to bed without recording new experiences you have had during the day and what you have learned. You can note down new ideas in a small notepad, quietly sit around with your exercise book or computer, or even, as some of us do, prepare an audio diary to listen to later and note down ideas to put into practice.

***Experience 7: Solving the problem of distraction**￼*

One of the problems I had when I was a student was that I was often distracted by issues and ideas that were sometimes different from what I was studying and which did not allow me to focus as I did not want to forget them. So three or four hours of study effectively ended up being only two hours of productive work. After a study session, I felt that for a good while, I had been wasting time and that made me angry with myself.

One of the best pieces of advice that I received from a friend was a method that she used: simply to study with a paper next to her, so that if she had an idea which distracted her from her studies, she would jot it down on the paper and set it aside. In this way, her mind was not occupied by trying to remember it. It was down on paper. When she had finished studying, she returned to her list and could turn her attention to what she had noted down.

> *As the years passed, I bought myself a small tape recorder which I usually carry around with me on my trips. This helps me to remember all that comes to mind, which may distract me from day-to-day matters, and later to listen to it quietly at home or the hotel where I might spend the night.*

I am discovering what I am good at

When I was 18, to finance my university studies, I began working in a company with a Personnel Department. There they deal with all areas linked to contracts, payroll and workforce administration. Gradually, over the years working in different companies, the very name of the department responsible for the people working for the company was also evolving.

It became known by a new name: the Department of Human Resources. It is a title that has become widespread and institutionalized, but it generated a certain amount of debate as some people would say that 'people' could not be called a mere '*resource*'.

The current name, and one which features in many companies nowadays, is the *Department of Human Capital Management*. And as always for the most critical, the idea of combining the word '*Capital*'' with 'people' has also become a bone of contention in some forums, although it is a term that is more accepted than being only a '*resource*'.

Lately, we are seeing a trend to refer to it as the '*Management of Talent*'.

In other words, people have moved from being just *'Personnel'* to becoming valued according to their *'Talent'*. Nowadays, we can find great treatises on Talent, and when they talk about hiring people, they talk about hiring Talent.

Perhaps, the evolution of the name of this department is coincidental or perhaps it is not, but it is true that the word appears in literature several centuries ago. Although in antiquity, *'Talent'* was a form of currency, it was used synonymously to mean skills and abilities that we possess and how we develop them.

In other words, for centuries we have been aware that we all have talents and we all have to cultivate them and make them productive (or as each person wants to call it), but not bury them. Therefore, we must be aware of what we consider our talents to be without feeling that we are being conceited in acknowledging it, because from a perspective of what I am, I will be able to improve, change or even transmit it with my example.

The 'I' who knows what I do well and, more specifically, what I do **not** know is important. This last point is a quality that is not often seen among friendship groups, professionals or in organizations. How many mistakes, wasted time and money would we have saved ourselves if we had only admitted at the start that we did not know something?

Tip: At 17, make a personal list of your talents, qualities or abilities that you have now. They will then develop, or you will think that you ought to have others, and therein lies true wealth: in being aware of what you have and to cultivate its development. Then at 27, 37, 47, ... we should review the list at least every 10 years to see how it has developed, how much we have improved and how we have in turn changed.

Experience 8: Basic quality in a job interview

From the first time I took part in a selection process for summer camp leaders at the age of 23 up to just two weeks ago for business development project managers in a European country, I have seen that over the years, people have become less inhibited about talking positively about themselves and about their qualities.

There is a balance to be struck, shall we say a delicate balance, between someone who finds it difficult to talk about himself and someone who only knows how to talk well about himself. Each person has to know how to position himself in each case. Obviously, the danger is that if a person is successful in a job interview, as a result of a list of good qualities, he must keep in mind that in his everyday work, they will be the first abilities that will be demanded of him and by which he will be assessed.

Therefore, it is very important to be honest with yourself and with others.

The 'I' who makes decisions

It is vital that we feel that we are able to make decisions appropriate to our age from the time we are children. Many 17-year-olds will have had to make a few decisions, while others will have made more.

Tip: For those who think that they have not made many decisions, I would suggest that they find their own reasons to do so, because making decisions often means making mistakes, but this is precisely what we have to do to succeed. At work, we are often asked to make decisions and we cannot do so without first having been '*trained in making decisions*'. I hope you do not have the experience that I once had.

Experience 9: Job interview silence

In 2007, I had to run an interview for a technical job in a department in the company for which I was working.

Among the candidates that we had to interview was a young woman who was 27 at the time. Among the questions and answers during the interview, I asked the candidate, as I did with all the others, to talk in-depth about her ability to make decisions by herself and to give an example.

I will never forget how uncomfortable it was because, at age 27, she did not know how to answer. She went blank. At first, I thought that it was because she was nervous, until she herself said that she could not remember any, except for one year when she helped her mother to organize the summer holidays.

The 'I' who participates

At 17 and beyond, it is a good practice to take part in everything that you can: activities organized by your school, in your area and trusted organizations, and even competitions.

They will help you explore who you are and you will also get to know other people with whom you may end up forging links for future friendships, or even with people you may meet in your future professional life.

Education as a base line

Some people see education as finite in time. On the contrary, many of us know that it '*continues*' throughout our lives. Can anyone imagine a doctor who does not keep up-to-date with the latest drugs to cure illnesses? Or a welder who does not learn new welding methods that have been developing over recent years? Can anyone imagine a teacher who does not keep up-to-date or study new teaching methods?

Training is a part of our lives.

You in this current generation have greater facility than those of previous generations because your day-to-day lives are based on learning, and trying out new programs and applications available for an infinite number of objectives.

However, we can still find people who say that they are too old to learn, but I say to you that your generation will never say that, because you have within you an enormous capacity to continue learning and to learn new things. Do not reject it. See it as a challenge and therefore you will enjoy it even more. This is perhaps an important difference between the past and present generations.

Study what you like most...

"Study what you like most because then you will be able to work in whatever you can put your hand to", is the statement I prefer to say to young people who ask me about what they should study. The most important thing, I always say, is to enjoy what you are studying because therein lies your vocation or special interest for the subject. That enjoyment will enable you to pursue all future paths in your studies and will allow you to deepen your knowledge in the area you like best.

Sometimes when you study, you may have one of the following experiences:

Experience 10: Difficulties in a subject

I know a woman who studied Law.

In her final year, she had problems in passing the Business Law component. She did not know how to study for it. The more time she spent on it, the worse it became because she could not grasp the concepts.

What happened was that she passed everything except this subject. She therefore had to spend the last summer completely dedicated to it.

She succeeded in finding a studying method and managed to pass, to the extent that she liked it so much that she later opened a Business legal consultancy firm. Years later, she travelled to the USA to perfect her English and is currently a partner at a law firm in which her main clients are foreign companies wanting to set up in Spain.

Experience 11: Skills in a different profession

A colleague of the lady mentioned above also completed her university studies in Law. In her final year, she linked it to another university course: Social Work.

When she entered the labour market in Law, she discovered other work opportunities in this secondary area of study that she had started. She decided to complete her studies in Social Work, and since then, she has never been short of work as a social worker in government organizations or in NGOs, not only because of her ability and training, but also because of her memorization and analytical skills, in addition to her overall legal training acquired in her studies in Law. Her Added Value is not just double, but triple: training in Social Work, training in Law and the skills acquired from the combination of the two fields of study.

When a young person begins his studies, university or otherwise, what basically he is doing is 'investing'. He supposes that he is studying something that will allow him to work in his field of study. But perhaps the scenario changes radically when he completes his studies, and what first appears to be a job opportunity may, later on, disappear or be transformed. The attitude with which he faces this challenge will determine whether he progresses or not.

Perhaps at the end of his studies, there is a huge financial crisis and work opportunities in the area he studied in his country may have disappeared. One has to be prepared for that.

Experience 12: Keep active during your studies

Here, I can give many examples, but I will focus on two.

I know a person who studied Philosophy and Literature. While he was at university, he was very active, working with various institutions and NGOs. Since he completed his studies, he has never lacked for work as a teacher in secondary school and further education in History and Philosophy. He is very well regarded by his students and the rest of the teaching staff. In addition, he writes books, promotes initiatives to encourage reading, and it is not rare to see him giving lectures in his sphere of influence.

I know another person who studied Veterinarian Sciences. While he was studying at university, he managed a sheep farm. His knowledge of business allowed him to find many business opportunities in various areas of food and beverage distribution. A few days ago, when I was discussing his career with him to include it in this experience, he told me that one of the aspects he valued most was his involvement in various NGOs, both as a student and later. He admits that introducing this 'other' perspective in his studies has been of great value, so much so that he is able to embrace current business initiatives from a more social and human perspective. Without intending it to be so, this approach

---

> *continues to enhance his prospects in many business ventures.*

Special personal space

Tip: Always have a space for you to '*tingle*'. I use the word '*tingle*' to describe the sensation that you have when you are fully aware that your mind and body are in a state of total passion. It adds to your enjoyment and the memories of this experience are those which, in the future, you will recall in order to feel better in times of difficulty.

We know that some people think that they achieve this level through insane means such as drugs or alcohol. But it is not true; they are unable to 'tingle' because they lack awareness. They simply seek escapism and, above all, ill-treat their own bodies. Those of us who have something that makes us *tingle* (in my case, when I go mountaineering), experience something that we call moments of 'Epiphany' in which we may have great ideas that will change our future.

Tip: When you are aware of what makes you tingle - walking, going to the cinema, playing chess, listening to music, cooking, yoga, Zen, running or whatever it is - pursue it and try to do it regularly. And moreover, if you do it with others, so much the better for you and your companions.

The 'I' who reads

It is fundamental. It would be impossible for me to describe everything that I have learned though reading, and even the feelings that I have experienced through books. I hope you all spend several years reading and feel that you need to do so. That will help you greatly in the future.

Tip: Read actively. Read with a pencil at your side or something that will allow you to note down interesting ideas so that, when you finish reading, you can revisit them because you will be able to apply many of them to real life.

Experience 13: Job interview - Reading

At job interviews that I had attended when I applied for a post and those that I have conducted myself with candidates throughout the years, it has been a routine practice to ask the candidate if he has read something lately. The interviewer does not focus only on whether the candidate has to think a lot about it, implying that he has not read or that it has been a long time since he has done so, but also on what kind of book he has read and, above all, how he describes it.

A month ago, during a job interview, there was a candidate that I liked a lot during the interview. When, in response to the question, he talked about the book he was currently reading with so much passion and ease, summarizing a complicated argument in just a few minutes, it reflected positively on his ability to analyze and to communicate.

We offered him the post there and then, and he accepted.

The 'I' who communicates in writing

As I do not exist in the world alone, I have to interact with others and therefore, I have to focus on my own attempts to communicate.

We currently have many methods of communication, benefitting from all the technical advances. Various IT tools allow us to do it on the computer, Tablet or mobile phone. Often, our use of language deteriorates owing to, among other things, our use of mobile devices for communication, especially when we abbreviate our words or use acronyms that sometimes we don't even know the meaning of.

Communication experts warn us about instant messaging applications. It is fine to abbreviate words; it is great fun. We have created a new language form and quite a few people understand me. Brilliant! What nice people we all are! But that is not real life.

Experience 14: Spelling

In real life, we have all seen colleagues who have failed important exams because of spelling mistakes; we have witnessed colleagues with administrative and secretarial duties dismissed because of repeated spelling errors; we have seen an engineer sidelined because of the

> *same problem and who was incapable of writing a good*
> *report.*

Spelling errors are not permitted on LinkedIn. While on Facebook and Twitter, it is not penalized, to have spelling errors on LinkedIn is like having spelling errors on your CV.

Tip: Exercise great care in your use of language. For example, if someone has spelling errors on his profile or even his CV, on professional social media which deal with cultivating contacts of quality and even companies looking for talent or to recruit staff, it will reflect poorly on his professional image when what they are looking for is just the opposite.

The 'I' who communicates in person

When I am communicating, I must focus on continuously improving my personal skills. Each person will need to recognise which of his personal skills are most necessary, based on the group or sector that pertains to them. Perhaps the most important skill, however, is the ability to listen.

It must be active listening, in which the speaker is aware that we understand him and that we are not just waiting for him to finish speaking to give him our comment or opinion; a listening exercise in which we give physical signs, nodding to confirm that we have understood what he has told us and to encourage him to continue speaking; a listening exercise in which, from time to time, we summarize what we have been told to show clear interest in what the speaker is saying and that we have understood it; but, more specifically, we should listen with sincerity.

As time goes by, you find people who demonstrate all the techniques for good listening, but instead of genuine interest, they do it for other motives.

Experience 15: The best bosses

After years of experience in companies and in non-profit organizations, you become convinced that the best bosses, heads of departments or coordinators are those who are the best listeners.

The 'I' who takes care of my body and cares for Health and Safety

Here, I will stop for our own professional good to deal with three aspects that are normally incorporated within the same department in organizations: Health, Safety and Hygiene.

Health

Without being excessive in professing the cultivation of the body, we must apply that adage *'mens sana in corpore sano'* to our everyday life. Practising sports, avoiding excesses of food, alcohol and, in particular, drugs, are the maxims that we should follow. I have seen young people of 19 and 20 years who cannot enjoy themselves unless they get into a drunken stupor, people who at 37 have had a heart attack caused by an excessive mix of stress at work and chaotic consumption of alcohol and tobacco.

__Experience 16: When to do sports__

A few days ago, a friend told me that he had gone out for a few hours of sport when, on his way, he came across a group of cyclists standing around.

When he approached them, he saw that one of them was lying on the ground. The ambulance, which had just arrived, had pronounced him dead at the scene. My friend told me that when he saw another of the men with the dead man crying, he asked him what had happened. The latter told him that it was his friend who had just retired the previous day and had decided to do a sport for the first time.

He had just had a heart attack.

Safety

In my professional career, I have worked in an oil refinery which, together with nuclear power plants, is among a group of installations requiring the highest levels of safety in the industrial sector. In these companies, it is as important to generate economic profits as it is to maintain maximum levels of health and safety. Moreover, if the second is not achieved in such chemical installations, they will be closed down.

It was a very interesting period that has left an enormous impact on me. In fact, I had the good fortune of working in an industrial plant where the safety of people was the priority within the culture of the organization.

When, occasionally, I see that basic protective measures for people are not maintained for some jobs, I wonder if they think about others.

Tip: We must always be aware of our safety and that of our colleagues, and do not put this safety unnecessarily at risk. We should be continuously reviewing risk prevention measures. Let us start at the home, assess where there are risks and do what we can to avoid them.

Experience 17: Question or situation

I know a father who, from the time his children were small and beginning to walk, used to play a game with them called 'Question or situation?'

His children already knew that if they said 'situation', their father would present them with a situation that could occur at that moment and ask them what they would need to do: what would they do if there were an earthquake, a flood or a crowd of people running to where they were standing.

What their father was trying to teach them was being treated like a game.

What is clear is that these children, from the time they were small, were being introduced to extraordinary situations that could occur and could affect their safety or that of others at any moment, and at least for a moment, they thought about how they would deal with them.

Hygiene

And hygiene, this is a subject that few people dare to mention. It is assumed that we all have a level of personal hygiene and there is no need to talk about it explicitly. The problem occurs when someone does not have it and is unaware of it, and no one dares mention it to them.

Experience 18: Personal Hygiene

Unfortunately, twice in my professional life, I have had the experience and in both cases, no one dared to say it explicitly to the person concerned.

Someone told me that he had a colleague with whom he shared an office, together with another. Such was the odour that in winter, they would open the window to 'ventilate' the room, as they would say. They were never able to tell him anything. He was an expert in his field, but the truth was that people were uncomfortable around him.

In the other case, it was a woman in a company who dressed very elegantly and was always very well made up, but if you had to talk to her at 8.30 in the morning, it was obvious that something was wrong. No one, not even her own boss, was able to say anything to her. I did not hear any complaint about her professional development, but when it was time to renew her temporary contract, they simply did not do it.

SECOND AREA OF GROWTH: GROUP

"Tell me and I forget. Teach me and I remember.
Involve me and I learn."
Benjamin Franklin

"Ask not what your teammates can do for you. Ask
what you can do for your teammates."
Magic Johnson

Second area of growth: GROUP

Unless you are an international spy or a keeper of a distant lighthouse, at your job in a company or any organization that you may decide to join, you are going to have to work with other people. The relationships you establish with other members of the group will clearly play a major role in your work, and may even bring about a change in you and others. The way we behave in the groups to which we belong will impact on the group itself and may help to build or destroy, to advance or hinder it. Therefore, when we are preparing to Add Value, we have to consider how we manage our relationships within the group.

Nowadays, groups are more virtual, not as physically present as they were before the explosion of the technological era. Some do not see them as groups, but the members themselves feel part of a collective and so I will treat them as they are: groups.

Some real-life experiences allow me to share with you today ideas that form the basis for routine behaviour in companies and organizations.

The group that protects me

Often the first feeling that we have in a group is one of protection. If anything happens to me, the group will protect me. If something goes wrong for me, it is absorbed by the group. If I don't want to think or make a decision, I follow the group.

And the following feeling concerns the group to which I belong: how they see me, how I see them, what I am offering to the group for it to go forward and overcome problems, or simply how to have a good time or to think about what will make the group happy.

One of the books, which have left its mark on me when I was young is the book *Illusions* (Richard Bach, 1977). The author uses a short story to share a series of thoughts. On the back cover, there was a single quote which spurred me to buy the book.

Reading

What would you do if God spoke to you directly and told you, 'I order you all to be happy while you are alive'? What would you do then?" the Master asked the multitude.[5]

The statement is very captivating because, regardless of what religious belief we profess (even if we have none), it is a song to humanity. Whoever believes in a Creator God, or simply that we are here for a purpose, might say that what we are all here for is to be happy. However, we have to study the phase carefully, given that it is in the first person plural, that is, it is not addressed to the individual as '*you be happy*', but rather '*you **all** be happy*'. The conclusion we could draw from this is that our concern should be for 'all of us' to be happy.

Tip: The first place to practise this is within the group in which we are involved. The closest group will be the family, then the group of friends, school mates, colleagues at work, at sports, in the area, in the city; and if we continue like that, we will end up where we started the lecture, with the fundamental objectives of humanity.

Share, broadcast, cooperate, be committed

Individually, these four words already have sufficient power. So if we now combine them and think of their effect as a whole, it would be like a sum of synergies, as if we were contemplating the four elements in nature (water, air, fire and earth) to explain what happens around us. In this case, these four words would form a solid foundation for the success of a group.

Tip: We should put all four into practice at the same time in our daily lives. If someone mentions only one of them, always try to combine it with the other three.

Experience 19: Quality of the 'Children of the Millennium"

A few days ago, I read an article in a magazine about the 'Children of the Millennium' - people born in a range of years around the year 2000.

Out of the four interviews with young people between 22 and 27 years old, three of them said that they see themselves as being different from previous generations and one of the most significant differences is that today, they are people who share more. They pointed to the fact that, in the face of shortages and the current economic crisis, they are finding that this is the way forward. They all agreed that this 'fact' is the Internet - the platform on which they share, and, through it, everyday life.

> *I am firmly convinced that the Internet offers room for improvement for people, which was not available before in the same measure. We are in a new era with many advantages because, whatever is created on the Internet (blogs, social networks ...), they all have one main objective: to improve something by involving everyone and to transmit it virally.*

This year, I have read a book called the *ZEN of Social Media Marketing* (Shama Kabani, 2013). The author makes some important suggestions for an Internet business. I will focus on one of the reflections she makes on social media. The Internet is seen as a new form of community. According to the author, *"There's collaborative thinking on Twitter at a level and in a form I've never seen before. Almost every day and often many times a day, a topic comes up that causes me, as a philosopher and simply a curious individual, to ponder a bit and then share the results of that pondering in the 140 character increments, or tweets that Twitter allows."*[6]

Of course we have different ways of understanding the word '*community*'. If we stick to the strict meaning of the word, someone could say that they are not real communities, which is totally superficial. My point of view is always constructive and I would advise those critics to understand the '*fact*' (the Internet) first, and then they will see the great advantages there are because, if the four words mentioned above in the title of this section are included in the word '*community*', then I think that we have already made significant social progress, especially if we are looking for a change for the better.

An observation on the world of social networks, which is important, relates to the fact that we ourselves have to be authentic. There may be a tendency to supplant our own personality because, at the end of the day, we sometimes use a non-visual form of communication, even to the point of creating our own avatar in order to live a parallel life. The problem with this approach is that if at some point someone or other discovers that it is based on a lie, then from that point on everything vanishes.

Experience 20: The consequence of lying

I know parents who have always told their children: the person who lies disappears, because no one will believe in you. It is as if you do not exist.

Tip: Based on what we have discussed above, after today's experience, if you have enjoyed it, make a viral transmission: publish it on YouTube, Twitter, Tuenti... tell your friends and family.

Make your life 'complicated'... it is worth it.

Contrary to the above statement, many of us have heard the phrase, *'don't complicate your life'*, *'it's not worth it'*. The message I bring to you today is exactly the opposite: yes, it is worth *'complicating'* our lives, especially if it is done within the group, through our interactions with others, which would enable us to bring about change together in order to Add Value. It is very important, therefore, to start thinking about others in the context of service and try to accept feedback on what we do.

The first step in 'complicating' life is to live it from the perspective of '*giving*' in our relationships with others. It is very important that we know how to be selfless in what we do; it is very important that we are not always looking to bring about a change for our own benefit in everything that we do.

In this section, I refer to the book, *Linchpin, Are you indispensable?* (Seth Godin, 2011). Whether you agree or not with the title chosen as a commercial hook to sell the book, I must admit that the tips that he proposes for our corporate interactions are magnificent. The author bases the improvement of our behaviour within organizations and groups on several pillars, one of which is specifically 'to give freely in whatever we do'.[7]

From a business perspective, the behaviour of people who only do something for rewards - an increase in salary or internal promotion - is eventually found out. In contrast, those who work with the view to giving their best efforts freely are the ones who, indirectly and without realizing it, make the greatest contribution to the group.

Tip: How do we train ourselves for this? The best way is to incorporate this idea of *giving* in our everyday life, within the family, among friends, or at work. As a young person, one of the best ways is to opt for voluntary work.

Voluntary work in itself generates change. Firstly, a person changes his view of his relationship with the world, and secondly, and perhaps more importantly, it changes the lives of those to whom the voluntary work is directed. At 17, in addition to training, let us consider volunteer work, as a fundamental pillar (obviously, as long as there are no financial necessities that might prevent us from devoting sufficient time).

There are many fields in which everyone, even a young person, can become involved as a volunteer. It will depend on his '*talents*' as we have mentioned earlier, his attitudes and abilities that are continually developing throughout his life, and of course, the aim of the voluntary work, at local level, community level, nationally and even internationally.

As with any job, it involves commitment, which is implicit within voluntary work at its very core. Therefore, I would say YES to Voluntary Work, but NO to any Voluntary Work. In each case, it must be done with commitment. Although I do not have a graphic image to express this, such as the drawings I showed at the beginning, I will leave you with a text that I used in a NGO training course I delivered 17 years ago. The title of the text is '*Involuntary Volunteer*'.

(See APPENDIX 1: Tale of the Involuntary volunteer (Involuntariamente voluntario)

Show appreciation

It is a very simple saying in this context, but it is one of the maxims of our relations with the rest of the group or organization to which we belong.

Tip: Let us always remember to thank others for what they do. In particular, let us say it to them because, by acknowledging it, I may imitate their good work and others seeing me will, in turn, do it; and so we end up spreading good behaviour if, from the outset, we understand that it is worth replicating.

Experience 21: Special Teacher, Special Action

When I was at university, we had a special teacher. We noted the difference from the outset. The first day of class, other teachers delivered classes in a relaxed and casual manner, introducing themselves and giving overviews of what the content of their subject during the course would be. This special teacher started speaking very softly in an almost shy manner and, after a very brief introduction, started the class. In fact, as fellow students would attest, on the first day, he had filled the entire board, and we several pages, with notes. Of course, we had not expected it as we were anticipating something much gentler on the first day.

What we discovered subsequently is that he was not like that. He was precisely the opposite, which was confirmed in the second lesson. He was energetic. He gave explanations looking directly at the students and waited to answer questions if there were any. He modulated the tone of his voice so that his classes would not be boring. He cared about the students. He was always positive when he recognized that we had not understood. I think that he knew that his subject was very difficult, and there was a time when we could not follow the lesson because we were lost. He was a very good teacher and taught subjects for several university courses.

I have a friend who, when he passed the last subject he had with this teacher, went directly to his office. As always, the door was open. He saw that the teacher was very busy working at his desk, and had not seen that he was standing in the doorway. My friend had to knock on the door a couple of times to get his attention. The teacher looked up and offered to help him. My friend went up to him, shook hands with the teacher for a couple of seconds, and told him that he was a very good teacher, explaining all the good things he had learned from him in the two courses in which he was a student. Finally, he thanked him.

The teacher had not expected it. My friend did not expect anything from his action. He simply thought that it was appropriate to thank him and did so. The teacher was disconcerted at first until, smiling broadly, he thanked my friend for his kind comments.

Years later, for professional reasons they met each other a couple of times and were happy to see each other.

Do we live in a bubble?

It is a question that many of us have asked at some time in our lives. We study, we interact with people who are very much like us. That is very good because we are part of a group which protects us and encourages us to excel and, what is even better, we know that beyond this bubble, there are more people.

Tip: We must grasp opportunities to interact with *'people outside the bubble'*. The bigger the bubble we create, the less of a bubble it will be.

Experience 22: Divergent

This is a totally personal experience that happened to me a few months ago when I went to the cinema with my wife and children. My older daughter at 14 had read the complete trilogy of Divergent, Insurgent and Allegiant. We were very much looking forward to seeing the first film, which was based on the novels written by Veronica Roth in 2011.

I went to the cinema without any expectations about what I was going to see since, when you go to see something produced for teenagers and young people, as an adult from the time you enter, and without knowing why, you put up a barrier for you assume that it is not going to be for you.

Imagine my great surprise when, from the beginning, I enjoyed the story - a futuristic view, according to which, society had become fragmented into closed groups. In this story, each group of like-minded people did not interact with any other, having been forced to choose a specific group to belong to. That society had compelled them to choose only one group. Many accepted the fact... until someone decided not to do so. The story obviously presents an extreme case, but it should make us consider to what extent we choose to live in a bubble in our

> *everyday life and not leave it, or allow ourselves to be boxed into a role.*
>
> *To what extent are we fighting to be 'divergent'?*

Three key expressions

I give you: *Thank you, I'm sorry* and *Please*. You do not know the power you get from saying them until you use them. Some people are incapable of saying them and others simply wait for them to be said.

We will show the quality of gratitude, humility and kindness which should accompany us throughout our lives.

At a work level, I have seen organizations where they are never said and others in which they are an inherent feature of collegial relations. Imagine which ones people enjoy most and add greater value.

Tip: From the beginning of personal development, we will try to use these magical words. They may change the other person, the group... or even create magic.

On basic assumptions

In all groups and organizations there are a series of ideas, modes, customs, values and behaviours which we normally refer to as *'culture'*. In his book, _Organizational Culture and Leadership_ (1985), Edgar H. Shein illustrates the point that *without a group, culture cannot exist, and without a certain degree of culture, in reality all that we can do is to talk about a number of people, but not of a group.*[8]

Many aspects of this culture are normally not written or stated (*'basic assumptions'*).

When a new person joins a group, be it a group of friends, school or university students, or work colleagues, if he does not know or is unaware of this *'assumption'*, it can lead to conflict. If, for example, we think that a group of friends greatly value the way their members dress or the way they behave according to certain external criteria, and as this is not normally written down, nor is it obvious, being unaware can greatly hinder the relationship of new people with such groups.

Knowing its basic assumptions enables the individual to get to know the group better and then, make a decision on whether to join or not, because of differing values. Specifically, knowledge of assumptions enables us to make a choice.

Basic assumptions are contained within our communications and often they prevent us from moving forward, be it in a negotiation, in sale or simply in the teacher-student relationship or with friends. If we see something blocking our relationship, we must use empathetic approaches to become familiar with the expectations of the other.

Often, we take it for granted that the other party knows and agrees to them, yet it turns out that they do not know, and if they had known, perhaps they would not have accepted them.

But if it were known what the other party had taken for granted in the relationship, which blocked progress, it would enable the other party to adapt to the communication, explain the lesson better to them, arrive at an agreement and even finalize a sale, or simply to reject it because it does not coincide with what they are thinking or need.

Second area of growth: GROUP

THIRD AREA OF GROWTH: OBJECTIVE

"There is nothing that human beings try to preserve as much, or manage so badly, as their own life."
Marcus Tullius Cicero

"Life is what we make of it."
Tibetan Proverb

"If you do not climb the mountain, you will never enjoy the scenery."
Pablo Neruda

Third area of growth: OBJECTIVE

The company you want to join or the association in which you want to begin working has a Mission, a Vision and a series of established objectives to achieve. We must understand them, confirm that they match our own and if they do, make them our own.

Let us be clear about where we want to go, plan how we are going to achieve it, be prepared to adapt in order to promote the objectives to be achieved and when we achieve them or not, evaluate them. Normally when we talk about objectives, we are also talking about time and money. That, we will leave for later.

Here are some thoughts for you to consider in order to align your objectives to those of the organizations of which you are a part, or simply to keep your objectives alive until you find a project that you are passionate about.

Where I want to go; where we want to go

As we mentioned at the beginning, our existence is based on two fundamental objectives which could be: to eradicate world poverty and achieve world peace. However our day-to-day lives must be based on more achievable goals.

Tip: Draw up a plan of personal objectives and even write them down. Perhaps, after the summer is a good time to do it or perhaps on 2 January is the best time (Forget any idea about 1 January).

First, it is useful to set out the areas in which we want to set goals: whether they are to do with training, sports, learning a new hobby, supporting an NGO, learning to play an instrument, composing a song, writing a book, setting up a company, or joining a political party. Objectives should be both short and long-term.

Tip: Every year, we should review long-term objectives in order to adapt the short-term ones. If I want to form a music group within two years, first I will have to know if there is an area of music that has to be reinforced and set short-term objectives to do so. Then I will have to see if there are enough members to form the group and set objectives accordingly; if I have the financial and other resources such as instruments, venues for rehearsals, and if not, set short-term objectives to achieve them. Then, I will have to achieve those goals and review them periodically. It is important to know what I want to achieve, or if it is a group objective, what we want to achieve; what means do I, or we, have to achieve it; the necessary resources and, above all, the deadlines for achieving goals.

Experience 23: Learning to plan

In my earlier life, we organized several camps for children and young people, some for a few days and others for two weeks. It was clearly an important moment for setting goals, developing them, achieving them and evaluating them.

The experience really begins in the planning phase, because one has to have a location, with sufficient requirements such as water or access; the children who come and the camp leaders. My motto has always been 'to plan as much as you can, because in the end, you always have to improvise', and the longer the time you spend getting all the information you need, the better the decisions you will make during improvisation.

Is success achieving the objective?

Once we have set out our objectives, we must decide if the only measure of success is the achievement of the objective. When you have a passion for mountaineering, you will appreciate this dichotomy more. A sense of accomplishment and enjoyment are not only realized by reaching the summit, but also by plotting your own route.

Tip: Enjoy every moment of the route we are taking to reach the summit of the mountain or the personal objective we have set ourselves, because we may discover that success lies in the journey itself, even if we do not reach the top.

On the journey, we exert ourselves, we have sensations, we experience unexpected situations which we have to overcome, we share the journey with our travel companions, sometimes they help us and sometimes we help them. It always brings us something. What is important, as those of us who have experienced complicated situations know, is being on the mountain, and not getting to the top, but returning safe and sound to the refuge or valley (or the 'glen' as they say in Scotland) from where we first started.

Achievement of the objective can be the same, and perhaps we may have to abandon it at any moment or change the objective during the process, but what is most important is to enjoy the journey, and if it is made with others, so much the better.

Flexibility and the ability to adapt: resilience

Linked to the above section, this is a quality we must have in our personal development. Resilience is the ability to return to an original state after being subjected to pressure. Resilience is also the ability to adapt to adversity, to confront it and emerge stronger from it. Things that we will not like are going to happen, as well as those that we will like.

A book that I read for the first time when I was 17 is the *Greatest Salesman in the World*, written by Og Mandino. If you have the chance to read the biography of the author, you will see that his life is a model of resilience. I very much enjoyed the various jams that the protagonist describes and the lessons that can be drawn from them.

I still do not know why one of the concepts, little mentioned in the book, has remained with me all this time, and that is *'everything will pass'*. [9]

With the passage of time, you realize that it does - the good as well as the bad. We must recognize that it will pass and, therefore, the ability to be flexible and to adapt goes hand-in-hand with the ability to accept that we cannot go under when things go badly; or stop being extremely alert when things go well, because things can sometimes go back to what they were before.

Tip: Enjoy each moment ('*carpe diem*', they would say in olden days), and be aware of each event that happens to us in life, with the knowledge that nothing is permanent.

Third area of growth: OBJECTIVE

FOURTH AREA OF GROWTH: MONEY

"Price is what you pay. Value is what you get."
Warren Buffett

"Don't think that money does everything or you are going to end up doing everything for money."
Voltaire

"If you know how to spend less than you get, you have the Philosopher's stone."
Benjamin Franklin

Fourth area of growth: MONEY

Money is important. Money is very important. You have to know what your parents do for you to be here. Ask at home about household expenses - how much does electricity, water, telephone cost, and the mortgage. Do the research! I am sure you have seen with your own eyes the efforts that adults have to undergo to earn money, and I am also sure that you value what your parents do.

The value of money

Once, as a young person, you are aware of the value of money, the effort that is required to get it and how much things cost, that is when money takes on a whole new meaning. And that meaning is the correct one, that is, it is merely an element to be administered, but one that should not to be treasured, because therein lies the true problem with money: its role changes.

To understand it, there is nothing better than a story. I recommend the story, _El Círculo del 99_ (The Circle of 99), which you can find on the Internet. There are many versions of the same concept shown in different ways but they all convey the same message.

Tip: Take care not to fall into the _Circle of 99_.

Money as a generator of wealth

Money has one very important function and that is, it creates its own value, generating employment, creating wealth in places where it is distributed. Of course, we are talking about quality employment. There are many examples of people who have pursued this aim in their business ventures, and it is precisely they whom we must acknowledge as very good generators of value.

In this section, I cannot resist talking about the experience I had four years ago when in the same summer I bought three different books on the topic of money. Although I do not believe in coincidences, that summer I would have had to change my mind because it was amazing that I could find three very different, yet so complementary, books in various places where I had been on holiday with my family.

The first was called *Banker to the Poor* by Muhammad Yunus (2008), Nobel Prize winner for Peace in 2006. I had occasionally seen references to his project, but until that summer I had not known the details and relished an initiative inspired in principle to create wealth among the poor.

A few days ago, as I was reviewing documents for today's talk, I noticed on the Internet that lately, it has generated heated debate with attacks from some quarters and defence by others.

Without going into the arguments, personally, I think that one can conclude that there was a very broad consensus in the international community concerning the original idea of this economist and subsequent banker. He was the creator of the microcredit system to support impoverished communities within the population, primarily in India where he lived, with the aim of strengthening entrepreneurship among people who did not have any access to economic resources.

The second book, and very different from the first, was the biography of *Warren Buffett*, written by Hagstrom in 2011, which portrays the life story of this financial investor. From this book and other sources, I have learnt that he is highly respected, famous not only for his successful investments, but also for his philanthropy.

In addition, his social commitment has led him to demonstrate his support for raising taxes for the rich, to announce that he will donate more than 90% of his fortune to different NGOs and foundations before he dies, and to be one of the people who invest most money to social causes.

It is interesting that, despite his great wealth, he can claim austerity since he continues to live in the same house that he bought in 1958 and is one of the lowest paid among directors. In fact, shortly after buying shares in Coca Cola and becoming one of its major shareholders, he criticized the large bonuses paid to its directors so that they would reduce them.

Today, from this biography, I highlight his idea of '*generating wealth in investment*', on a long-term basis, with the intention of adding value, in areas that bring about wealth. I consider his idea the opposite of mere speculation, which is, namely, to get huge profits in the shortest time possible, without adding value.

The third book from that summer was: *Rich dad, poor dad* by Robert Kiyosaki and Sharon Lechter (*2008*). [10] To explain the different ways people manage money, the authors tell the story from the viewpoint of two young people who analyze the way each of the parents handle money.

In the first case, one of the fathers, despite his high level of university studies and doctorates, is always burdened by money problems; while in the other, the father with less education manages money from a diametrically opposed perspective. The first enters what the authors call '*the rat race*' in which the more money you earn, the more you spend and the more become indebted; while the other does not spend more than he earns, saves some of his money for a rainy day and makes profitable investments.

Although the book almost reads like a manual on how to be rich and perhaps puts forward an argument about the rich and the poor, which differs from my way of looking at society, I suggest reading the book for training on how to manage money from an early age. Indeed, it would be a very good idea to include money management as a subject for 17-year-olds.

Tip: Individuals (or their families) should manage their finances as if they were a company: analyzing income and expenditure, debts and that profits they want to have, what they are going to do with them and even before they get them, how they are going to prepare themselves for the next crisis (managing savings, minimizing expenditure, or hiring staff). Depending on the money you or your parents have, you may be able to do voluntary and/or paid work, and even the two at the same time. Many of us have done it.

I finished the summer with a different idea about creating wealth and on today's theme: Adding Value. Here we have a great international investor who leads a modest lifestyle and invests in the long-term whenever it may generate wealth; a banker in India who is personally and professionally committed to the disadvantaged, providing them with financial alternatives; and finally, a proposal on how to manage our personal finance - our own income, expenditure and finances.

Low cost style? Lean Management?

These are the in-words we encounter in everyday life, but they are just another way of talking about a style of living that has been practised for many centuries by those who effectively manage money: limit spending or we could say: eliminate what is superfluous, find and get rid of waste.

Everyone in their personal lives should think about it, but it is a fact that, in this period of crisis we are experiencing, all those people, organizations and companies that have learnt how to maintain a basic level of expense management during periods of plenty, are the ones that are more easily able to rise above the crisis and continue to add value to society. Those who have not done so... well, we have seen the outcome in the news, and even those people who have lived above their means.

And ... those who do not have money?

Tip: In addition to creating wealth, employment and managing money efficiently, when we talk about money, we must also ask ourselves about what we think about or what we do with those who do not have it.

The first reason for this question lies in the fact that we could be people who may not have money, and it is only then that we begin to see the world in a different way.

If we consider that the circumstances of those who do not have it arise from some kind of social injustice, then we always have recourse to supporting those structural changes deemed necessary to fight against injustices. But if by chance, at some point in our lives, we think that they do not have money because they have not worked hard enough, or even because they are lazy, we begin to think that they deserve what they get. At that moment, at that precise moment, I suggest that we stand in front a mirror and despise the person we see in front of us.

Our added value must be from a global perspective, and we can only deal with this global perspective if we consider all social sectors, especially the most disadvantaged.

We must take into account the impact of our economic actions on this last group - purchasing goods or services, where they come from or where they are produced because the sustainability we seek is not only economic, but also social and environmental. A negative impact on the environment means greater poverty; unjust social policies will lead to more poor people.

Tip: After everything that has been discussed above, let us consider that each time we have a profit, we share part of it with those who do not have. Let us each find a way, and seek opportunities to put it into practice, not as a form of almsgiving in order to have a clear conscience, but as a commitment to others with whom we share the present and part of the future, as a global commitment and as one more way to Add Value.

Network of Stakeholders

"A successful company is never successful by itself. It is successful because it has built a superior network of stakeholders, all of whom have a stake in the business and its outcome. Satisfying the stakeholders - ensuring that they all feel rewarded - will often lead to higher long-run profitability than when the company just focuses on trying to maximize short-run profits of the shareholders."[11] (*Marketing 3.0*, p. 103, Philip Kotler; Hermawan Kartajaya and Iwan Setiawan, 2010).

This statement, taken from the new trend in marketing, demonstrates that business companies are clearly being steered towards global rewards, and not only individual ones. Years ago, the aim was to sell the product and get maximum profit. That practice has led to many social problems that we see everyday.

Today, companies should focus on the rewards that not only shareholders get, but also what employees, suppliers, clients and the people around them - all of whom we call 'stakeholders' - receive.

With regard to this topic, it does not take a genius to know that a company must achieve economic profits to continue operating. What makes the difference today is that for these profits to be sustainable, the company, organization or group must consider the interests of the greatest number of stakeholders with whom it has a business relationship and try to satisfy their expectations.

Not everyone will be satisfied, but if we consider everyone and try to satisfy most of them, then the probability for success will be greater. And if, in considering those who cannot be satisfied, either because these stakeholders demand the impossible or because there aren't sufficient resources to satisfy them, at least knowing about this risk enables you to set up measures to control it.

"I went to business school and I apologize."

This is the title of a book I read recently, written by Florence Noiville (2009). She takes an interesting retrospective look on how we have arrived at this economic crisis which has had huge repercussions owing to, among other things, the fact that many professionals responsible for economic and financial decisions were ready for their moment in the sun and were not building for the future.

She describes the need for business schools to teach more *"Humanities: Philosophy, Psychology, Human Sciences, Economic History and Ethics. In short, true knowledge, not incorporeal techniques."*[12]

Reading

"...I had a dream. An economic-fiction dream. I am in the campus. It is the year 2019. I recognize it all: the exit to Vauhallan, the classroom building, the park. However, I have the impression that something has changed, although I cannot say what. The school is not exactly the same, but neither is it anything else.

A student suggests I attend a class in his specialty 'Poverty'. Poverty? Yes, he explains to me. Now, each specialty in this course corresponds to an issue in society: The Environment, Employment, Health Care, Poverty, ... I am dumbfounded. Have the classical options like Finance, Marketing or Strategy, disappeared? No, he answers. They are present in all the classes, but they have been put in to deal with the problems besetting the whole of society.

"I know that in the 20th century, it was the exact opposite. But we believe that it is precisely this absurd inversion that has disconnected education from the real world, and caused the 2008 economic catastrophe. This, we have learned in History. Moreover, we are encouraged even more to help solve them..."

Suddenly, it is interrupted. The teacher has just come in and starts a case study.[13]

Tip: Those of you who study Economics or work in jobs in which you have to deal with Business and Business Administration, try not to disconnect yourselves from real life, from the problems of society.

The last economic crisis that we are still experiencing had its origin clearly in the distortion of the principles of money management: selfishness, not thinking of others, focusing only on forms of profit at the expense of those with fewer economic, social or cultural opportunities

.

FIFTH AREA OF GROWTH: TIME

"Those who make the worst use of their time are the first to complain of its shortness."
Jean de la Bruyère

"For all evils, there are two remedies: time and silence."
Alexandre Dumas

"We must use time as a tool, not as a couch."
John F. Kennedy

Fifth area of growth: TIME

We often hear many more treatises about how to manage money than how to manage time. The truth is that it should be the other way round. We should concern ourselves more with the latter, among other reasons, because the first will depend on how we manage the second. In companies, they are looking for the best people for management, especially in how to manage the use of time.

Fifth Area of growth: 'Time'. *Time as an asset*

We have to see it as such, as an asset which has been given to us since we were born. Whether we are the ones to decide or whether we allow others to decide what to do with our time, how we use it will determine the management of the asset.

I say asset, because it is not a liability. Allow me this accounting analogy. A *liability* is something that is owed, which always has to be settled. In contrast, an *asset* is something that we have and which allows us to invest, create value and, above all, wealth (which I have already mentioned in the chapter before). Therefore, our time must be seen as an element that allows us to create wealth and to add value. How much time do I dedicate to each area of my life?

For example, there are some who think that time management means not doing sport and they miss a game or training session because they have an exam the following day. Instead, they ignore the truth that practising sports generates endorphins and these hormones help us to be more active with a greater attention span, apart from the fact that they fail to honour their commitment to the coach and the rest of the team.

If a day of studying is not productive, leave it… leave it immediately, and go out and do some sport for then you will return with a clear mind. Contrary to what you may think the first time it happens to you, it will help you to make better use of time.

Experience 24: Prisoner of a thief of time

Many years ago, we organized a dynamic group session for children of 12 to 13 years of age as a leisure time activity. It was one evening in July, at a beauty spot in the Pyrenees, which was sufficiently protected from the cold to allow us to have a quiet and friendly evening.

The children were asked to draw a circle on a sheet of paper provided for the activity. The circle represented the time they dedicated to the various activities they did during the week. They had to divide the circle into portions, as if they were cutting a cake, corresponding to the amount of time they spent on each activity.

As always with these exercises, what is truly interesting is the discussion that is generated at the end and the comments on the development of the exercise. When it was discussed in the group, we had to point out to some that there should be a 'portion' , at least one third of the time approximately, needed for sleep. After a few necessary adjustments, we shared what we had done.

What struck me most at that time (and I have thought about it a lot throughout my life, and right now I see it in

---

how my children allocate their time) was the amount of time they spent looking at TV, to 'see what was on'. We have to remember that, 25 years ago, there was no Internet or tablets. That is, if we compare the past to the present, we have to look at the amount of time dedicated to 'seeing what is on' the media available to them. On that occasion, some children mentioned that they watched at least 20 hours of TV a week. Some had their breakfast in front of the TV; when they returned home from school, they would have a snack in front of the TV; they did their homework in front of the TV; and at weekends, they could spend entire evenings in front of the set.

Why did it make such an impact on me? It was somewhat personal.

At the time, I was in my second year at University, and listening to the children that night, I identified totally with them. Although older than they, deep down, I was doing something similar. In fact, I had to admit to myself that I had failed that year and I had to repeat the year because of the issue of time management linked to, among other things, the TV.

In those days, I was one of those who said, "I'm going to watch TV a while to relax, and then I'll start studying." Mainly, after eating when I got home from classes, I would watch a series that I will never forget - Falcon Crest. At the end of it, I was incapable of studying. In fact, I was so unfocused that for a half an hour after the end of the series, I was incapable of sitting down to my books, and when I did, I could not concentrate. The rest of the afternoon, I was so busy with other activities that I could not find enough time to study.

Watching TV, and now videos on the Internet or simply surfing the Internet to watch things do not help you to study. In fact they do quite the opposite.

I found this out too late and I could not catch up on the subjects enough to pass the exams.

Fortunately, from the second year onwards and until I finished university studies, my relationship with the TV and those things that could distract me from my studies changed.

Thieves of time

The first time that I had heard or read something about the concept of the *'thieves of time'* was when the book <u>Momo</u> by Michael Ende fell into my hands. Those men in grey, who steal your time, do it so well that you do not realize it- a beautiful metaphor for something that is so important.

The second time was when, in my professional life and on a course for directors in the multinational company for which I worked, the presenter spoke about this concept. He told us that when we work, we are subject to constant attacks by *'thieves of time'*, and to be able to perform our duties properly, we have to identify them.

When you are working and the computer is your work tool, one of the great *'thieves of time'* is the email. There are people who don't know how to control themselves. As soon as an email arrives, they stop what they are doing, open it, read it and even reply.

Many of us have it set up so that emails are received at the same time as they are sent. Is this necessary? Would it not be more efficient to receive them after a certain time, say every half an hour, every hour? Or, instead of setting up the computer, are we not capable of exercising will power and simply not open emails when they arrive?

Tip: Decide whether the email is our *'thief of time'* and whether we should or should not, look at or open emails during a specified time, or leave them until after we have finished the work that we are doing.

Someone may say, "*Yes, that is all very well, but I have a boss who gets angry if you don't answer his email immediately.*" To this person, I say: either change your boss or mention it to him and explain that this habit is a *'thief of time'* and you cannot answer emails the moment you receive them.

Of course, the new *'thief of time'*, we carry about with us in our handbag, in our jacket or shirt pocket, and in the most extreme case I have seen: permanently in our hand. As you can guess, I am referring to the mobile phone or Smartphone, and everything associated with programs of instant messaging, social networks and various *'instant'* applications which allow me to see messages from the *'outside world'*.

It is important to check whether this is another *'thief of time'* or not, and what activity or commitment it prevents me from doing appropriately because it distracts me or simply keeps me from the work I am doing.

Other *'thieves of time'* - telephone calls, other people calling you unexpectedly when you are studying or working. We have to identify and deal with them appropriately so that they do not affect the action of adding value in what we are doing.

How we use other people's time?

Not only do we have to be concerned about our own time, but also other people's. People do not like to be disturbed when they are studying or working. Therefore, the first thing I have to do when I interrupt someone is to apologize because, at that moment, I am a *'thief of time'* for him.

And the second is to be brief in my communication with this person. We all know friends, family or work colleagues who do not know how to be brief. They go on for more than is necessary and are incapable of summing up or getting to the point.

Tip: When we address others, let us remember how we feel when they communicate with us, and then make a big effort to keep it short. If I can say something in seven words, why say it in seventeen?

On the other hand, if at some time you have a role or a job as a supervisor of people or teams of people, then this section is most relevant to you. If we have to manage other people's time, we need to have as much information as possible about them, the resources we have and the environment we have to work in to make decisions.

This is a part of good leadership and being trained to perform this role well and to treat people appropriately may be important. From our student days on, we have to work in groups, use our abilities to deal with others and to achieve objectives together.

One's own experience acquired from youth, as well as leadership training, will also enable us to add value when managing teams.

Time is a resource that is given to us

Unless we have been born into a rich family, we are not born with money. Our parents give it to us and later, we earn it when we begin to work. In contrast, time is something that is given to us when we are born. It is ours from then on for the rest of our lives.

There will be things that society itself will urge us to do, and it is then when we should have enough discernment to verify if it is we who are choosing what to do with our time or if it is our environment, or even, if we are allowing ourselves to be manipulated like puppets.

There is time, let us make good use of it and, if it is being used to add value or to train us to add value, so much the better.

Time which no one can take away from us

At the risk of repeating myself, it is worth reiterating a concept I mentioned earlier in this section. We should have something that makes us '*tingle*', something that serves like a lever to help us relax, have fun, and to shield or support us during moments of sadness or unease.

Tip: time is something that no one can steal from us. Let it be hardwired into our lives, let us maintain this commitment to ourselves to have it. Let us agree with others about having this time, if we need our parents, brothers/sisters or our partner to support us to relieve us from some obligations. It is important. It is also important that we do the same for others who ask us when we are on the other side of the fence, and it is we who are the parents, brothers/sisters or partner and it is the other person who requests it.

Experience 25: Studying with four quarters

I know a person who at 37 decided to go back to study while he was working. For four years, he was able to combine work, studies and family life. Indeed, it is during this period of study, that two out of his three children he has with his partner were born. It was a challenge for this person and more so for his wife. Of course, it was a commitment for the two of them to manage time so that he could study.

While he was at university, he would study at night. However, on this second occasion when he went back to study, after a hard day at work and family obligations at night, he altered this habit and got up early in the morning to get a couple of hours study before going to work.

For the weekend, he made an agreement with his wife to divide the weekend into four quarters: two mornings and two afternoon/evenings of eight hours each quarter.

The agreement was that for two quarters he would study and for the other two, he would spend time with the family.

He succeeded in completing his studies. The most significant development, however, is that while he was studying, one of the worst economic crises occurred. Many people lost their jobs, but this person continued to add value to his company during his studies and afterwards, because he was able to bring the new ideas he had learned into his workplace.

This is only one example, but fortunately within the circle of people with whom I interact, there are many in that age group - between 37 and 47 - who have undertaken studies or adapted to the changing economic environment, or simply for personal pleasure.

And the common thread in all of these cases has been the appropriate management of personal and family time.

Surplus time, what do we do with it?

Do I really have surplus time? We have all lived side by side with colleagues at college, university and at work who are always busy and we see that they make maximum use of their time. They got good grades, took part in sport, helped in the family, did other activities, and we even saw them around at some party with friends. These people have the greatest impact on us with regard to time management.

Let us seek them out, observe them and learn from them.

Experience has shown me that the more free time you have, the less you make good use of it. If you have little free time, you will make maximum use of it, so that, yes you will have some time left over. I have often been told that *"If you want to get something done, give it to a busy man."* It is absolutely true! I have proven it. When I have asked someone to do something, one way or the other, it has been done.

SIXTH AREA OF GROWTH: PROGRESS

*"Life is like riding a bicycle. To keep your balance you
must keep moving."*
Albert Einstein

"80% of success is just showing up."
Woody Allen

*"Every failure teaches a man something, if he will
learn."*
Charles Dickens, (Little Dorrit).

Sixth area of growth: PROGRESS

Companies, organizations and groups progress, and its members have to be aware of it. Often, this is in spite of the environment and in many other cases even the people who make up these bodies, because they too can be genuine barriers to progress. Fortunately, most of the time, it is the people who succeed in moving their companies forward.

Society has developed. Even though there are things that we may like more than others, we cannot deny that if we are not part of this progress, we will not be able to complain or express regret. Using the metaphor employed at the beginning of today's talk, we can choose or not choose to 'get on the train', which will always be moving.

Things were better in the old days ...

Apart from being a song a few years ago, the title is after all... a lie! Never, never let yourselves be fooled by statements like *'before, things were better...'* or even *'nowadays, people don't know how to make good use of time like they used to '*. It is far from the truth. Each period in time has its own issues and the ones today are different from those of previous generations.

The approach on which today's talk is based is this: "*YOU ARE LUCKY TO BE LIVING IN THE PERIOD IN WHICH YOU ARE LIVING NOW*", and I would even add that: "*ALWAYS LIVE YOUR LIFE BY ADDING VALUE TO THE FULLEST!*".

We are at the beginning of the 21st century where there are endless possibilities, as there were also in the past.

Today, opportunities to share information, conversations, images and videos open up many more areas of development to us.

Tip: Take advantage of all the opportunities you have in the time you are living.

Look to the future

A few years ago, when I joined the management team of a multinational company, I had the good fortune to attend a course on Negotiation. I was only 33 years old and the fact that a company invested in my training was something special, and I greatly appreciated it. The course was in Madrid. The consultant who led the course seemed to have a lot of experience in this area, especially in the way he delivered it and inspired us by the experience we were undergoing.

He gave us good strategies to deal with different kinds of negotiation scenarios we could encounter in our everyday work. He will never know the effect that the course had on me. It was not only the concepts that he conveyed or the experience we had; it was also the book he recommended: *Emotional Intelligence* (Daniel Goleman, 2002).

A few days after the course, I bought and read it. I admit that, at first, it was a struggle to absorb the basic concepts introduced in the first half, but this tendency that some of us have to finish something once we have started, spurred me on to continue reading. Fortunately, I did it because the second part of the book was fantastic - full of enthusiasm and, in particular, the great concept that he introduced had a great impact on me.

Without going too much into its principles, I want to share one of the conclusions that it explores, or perhaps the one I wanted to understand: that our emotional intelligence is directly linked to our capacity to overcome on-going frustrations, among other things.

As children, we get frustrated when we are not given all the sweets we ask for; as young people, if the results in an exam are not what we expected; when we are managing a business or social project and we do not get what we are aiming for at the first attempt.

So, while we need to know that in life we will encounter many occasions in which the outcome will be different from what we expect, perhaps the most important message of today's experience is that we should not be deterred from trying again.

Experience 26: Creativity on New Year's Eve

This is an experience that a couple had a few years ago during the Christmas festivities. At the time, they had three young children between 4 and 9 years of age. They had decided to have a family dinner for New Year's Eve at their home to which they had invited family members, among them uncles, aunts and grandparents of the children. The family of five in total had organized the dinner for up to 12 people with great care, and completed all the decorations and preparations to bring in the New Year, with games for the start of the evening. The children were very excited.

However, owing to unforeseen circumstances, six family members called to say that something important had come up and they could not attend.

The parents found themselves in a dilemma with the three children who, if they did not do anything, would be sad at the end of the old year and at the start of the new one.

With an innovative idea, the parents called the children together and told them that although they had expected 12 people to dinner, only 6 were definitely coming. So, they were going to do something about it so that there would be 12. What they decided was that each of the children, together with the three adults who were dining, would create an 'avatar'.

They went out to buy balloons, sticks, fabric and other implements so that in the evening, before dinner was served, each person would tie a stick to his chair with another stick across it to hold the fabric which they draped over it. At the top of the long stick, they attached a balloon.

Each child and adult had to draw a face for the avatar on the balloon being used as the head and, with the implements they had, to disguise the avatar. Then, they had to explain who and what the avatar was, how they behaved and what they liked to do to celebrate the New Year, of course not forgetting the moment when the avatars talked about their hopes for the New Year.

The dinner for 12, in which half of them were avatars made up of balloons, sticks and fabric, was a great

> *success, with a difficult situation being overcome and managed.*

Striving for continuity is the key component of many of the successes achieved in life. It is said that Thomas Alba Edison had many failures before securing an incandescent filament which produced what he wanted, and from which, electric light was invented. The statement, *"Many of life's failures are people who did not realize how close they were to success when they gave up,"* is attributed to him.

To throw in the towel is very tempting, especially when failures keep happening. But, it is precisely the chain of failed attempts that can lead us to success.

Benjamin Franklin, one of the main contributors to the Constitution of the United States, had a life full of successes, preceded by many early failures which led him to his objective. The statement attributed to him, *"I didn't fail the test, I just found a hundred ways to do it wrong,"* amply explains this way of thinking.

We should not be afraid of failure; but what we should be afraid of is not trying. In fact, a few days ago I was reading an article in a magazine in which it explained that in some places, they are currently *'paying people to make mistakes'*. It was a difficult concept to understand if you did not read more of the article in which it described that they are setting up research and innovation centres to allow people to make mistakes so that they will try again.

Perhaps this may be the basis of something that we will talk about later when we get on to creativity.

Don't be concerned, be constructive

Another statement that we hear a lot in our working life is '*I am concerned that...*'. When someone says, or worse, writes in an email to others that he is concerned that something is happening or not happening, he is only communicating his passivity.

In our work, we find ourselves with thousands of people who are experts in '*being concerned*' and in particular, in '*highlighting where there are problems*'. We have colleagues who come to a meeting and, for their presentation, announce that they have found a problem.

The issue is that once they say it, if you observe them closely, you detect that they are gloating over the '*great discovery that they have made*'. They even look at the others as if to say, "*Be impressed. I have found the problem!*"

The drawback for them is that sometimes they do not realize that we have already seen the problem and are thinking about the next step - which is to look for solutions.

Experience 27: Be Constructive

During the time I worked at a company, I had a unique experience which has had a lasting impact on me. At 27 years of age and assistant to the Head of the Division managing a project, I sent an email to the project manager of the company contracted to build the

---

installation. We had agreed to deliver in less than a month.

I sent an email and I felt very proud of all that I had written. I had presented the problem that I had discovered, with technical and planning information to support my argument. With such an email, I felt sufficiently justified to attach a copy to my manager, the heads of other departments and even to the Head of Department.

Such was my excitement when a couple of hours later, when I checked my email inbox, I saw that one from the Head of Department had arrived. As I was opening it, I was sure that he was going to congratulate me for the document that I had just sent him.

What I read did not make me angry, or disappointed or even fearful of authority; rather it led to a very significant shift in how I deal with my relations with others. The text of the email said: "You are not paid to be concerned, but to be constructive." I read the email that I had sent again, and I had copied him in it and saw that I had started with the phrase: "I am concerned that the project will not arrive in time..."

Since then, every time I hear or see that phrase in verbal or written communications, I remember this experience and wonder what the communication would have been like if, instead of putting 'concerned', I had written 'how can I help'.

Obviously, in groups and organizations, there is a need for people who can spot problems, but they are not the people we are looking for.

Tip: We need people who can work on finding the problem, analyze it and then propose solutions.

Experience 28: "We have problem!"

I once knew a manager who, when one of his employees entered the office excitedly, saying in a loud voice: "We have problem!"

The latter was invited to leave the office and come back with two or three solutions, unless he had already done so and he could think of nothing else.

Create the conditions to have Good Luck...

Perhaps this is the book I have bought the most and given away the most. Until this moment, I have never spoken to writers or received anything for the publicity that I have given them. However, I have to acknowledge that when something is good, you have to share it. If it were a phrase or thought, I would use the various options that the Internet and social networks provide us, but a book is a book. You have to read it, lend it or give it to others.

In 2007 at the company for which I was working, they put me in charge of two different offices in the same country, a thousand kilometres from each other. They were two different teams with different cultures and forms of working. In total, there were some seventeen people.

That Christmas, I gave each one of them a copy of the book _La Buena Suerte_ (Good Luck) by Alex Rovira and Fernando Trías de Bes, because we all have something in common. Later, on six more occasions, I gave it away to different friends and family.

The first time I read the book, I thought it was a nice story. The second time was when I was 37, and the effect was far greater than on the first occasion. Especially because of its grand message: _"Good luck only comes if we create the conditions for it."_[14]

Even though, perhaps, the opposite has greater impact, I see this behaviour in many people everyday - people who always say that they have 'bad luck'. There are people who say that there is neither good or bad luck.

I say that those of us who were born in a developed civilization in which there is no war, where human rights are not continuously under threat, where the family has sufficient means to feed us and even allow us to study, then, we must say that we are _lucky_.

Hence, we must aim for perfection even to the point of Good Luck because somehow or other, we ought to feel compelled to move forward and add value in this world in which _'because of luck'_ we are living, especially to make life better for those we think have had 'bad luck'.

At school, the same thing happened. There were schoolmates who told themselves that they were unlucky when they failed an exam or when things did not work out as they wanted.

I liked to study those students who, when leaving an exam, focused on what they did not do well as a way to deepen their knowledge to improve for the next exam.

We have all met the '*unfortunate student who is always unlucky*', but it is usually because they say it to themselves and 'share' it with others so that they will feel sorry for them.

This is the attitude that often gets in our way and does not allow us to move on. When something does not work out well or the result is simply different from what we wanted (an exam, an interview with someone, a project, a conversation with a family member or a job), if we stop for a moment and, before blaming it on bad luck, we say to ourselves that we are lucky to have learned something from the experience, this small step forward which we have discovered perhaps because of what has happened or by a simple approach to someone else, would take us down another avenue.

As we said beforehand, Thomas A. Edison did not simply have '*Good Luck*'; his was a consistent and continuous process of overcoming difficulties, of creating conditions so that in the end this '*Good Luck*' would appear. This is what he, and millions and millions of us since, called '*Electricity*'.

Justify your limitations ...

Another statement, that has made an impact on my life, comes from the book <u>*Illusions*</u> by Richard Bach, which I have mentioned earlier. After reading his great work

Jonathan Livingston Seagull (1986) a short time ago, I thought that I was going to like everything he had written.

With _Illusions_, I did not have the same reaction at first, as I had with the other book. Initially, the story he used to get his message across left me incredulous, but very soon it began to grab my attention.

But, it was not until I came across the sentence: _"Argue for your limitations, and sure enough, they're yours"_.[15] It was unbelievable because I found myself saying that there were things that I did not do simply because I told myself that I could not do them for one reason or another, which sometimes was an excuse. However, most of the time, saying it showed me that I was justifying to myself limitations which did not exist.

I began to look around, at my friends and companions, and everyday I saw the phrase reflected in many, who, like me, did not try something because they imposed their own limits on themselves.

If you want to enter higher education, start up a business, set up a NGO, or plan a mountain ascent, you must have a clear idea of the constraints of the venture you want to start.

To climb the highest mountain in the Alps, if it is essential to have suitable physical preparation, I can justify to myself that I cannot do it or I can be aware of this limitation and try to overcome it, in this case, with the appropriate training.

To study at university, if my family cannot give me sufficient funds and, what's more, I have to help in the family business, I can consider several options or, as many others have done, work and study at the same time. It is precisely these people who set an example for us by their way of looking at life. They are the ones who bring about changes. What would have happened if Martin Luther King had justified his limitations in the era in which he lived purely because of the colour of his skin? How many other leaders and thinkers have broken those constraints and taught us to forge on ahead?

After finishing this book, I re-read the first book of the author, *Jonathan Livingston Seagull,* in which he describes an individual who always tries to go beyond the routine, someone who, as cited in the back cover, *"gains special pleasure in doing something well, someone who divines something more than his sees, someone who prefers flying to finding food and eating."* There is a very beautiful moment in the book in which Jonathan, the protagonist, says to Fletcher, one of his disciples: *"The trick, Fletcher, is that we are trying to overcome our limitations in order, patiently."*[16]

Need to understand the value of 'work that serves no purpose...'

Many people only know how to do something if they get something else out of it. They are incapable of doing something without having a vested interest. Here, I have to mention that sometimes we have to do things which seem to 'serve no purpose'. The reason is clear: the very phrase is a fallacy because what, for some, appears to be useless, serves a purpose for others.

The problem is that if we do not first try this *'activity'* when we are young (doing things that may appear to have no purpose), then in our daily working life, we could run the risk of not progressing in our tasks or even on projects that may have an enormous impact in bringing about a significant change in society.

There are people who are incapable of undertaking task, jobs or activities if they do not see the *'fruit of their labour'*. Those of us, accustomed to working on long-term projects, know that we may not see the outcome of our work until very much later, we may never see it ourselves, or perhaps, it may never be seen within our generation.

Experience 29: Useful work?

When we were between 17 and 19 years of age, we would go out as a group to small villages in the mountains in the summer to help the elderly in farm work, to help out in the town or simply to be with them.

A close friend, who was at one of these villages told me, that in the morning a group of boys and girls would meet with the group leader responsible for planning the day's activities. Everyday they were assigned a task which caused great perplexity in the group: to clean the streets after the cattle drive each morning.

One day, one of them asked the leader, "Why do we have to do it, seeing that the next day it will be dirty again?" He went on to suggest that they should do it every two or three days. The group leader, who was twice their age, remained silent for a while and, with a gentle smile, looked directly at them and calmly told them that

---

> *they had to value 'useless work'. They said nothing and*
> *they were assigned the task again.*
>
> *That day there was a look of satisfaction on the faces*
> *of the elderly who lived in that small town, to have the*
> *streets clean every afternoon, to be able to take a walk, to*
> *sit down and talk among themselves or play cards.*

Why do we fall down?

In this section, I want to mention what I had seen in a film a few years ago. In it, there was a father with his children on the street. One of them tripped and fell on the ground.

After checking that he had not been hurt, with a glance he let his dad know that he was OK. His father then asked him, "*Why do we fall down?*" The son, still bending over, answered him, "*to get up again.*" This scene in the film was so charged with meaning that I have always recalled it when there were difficulties in studies or at work.

We have to move forward. We know that we will fall, we will stumble, we will fail, a project will not succeed, a relationship with someone will not be as we had hoped, but all this cannot prevent us from trying again and moving forward. Obviously, everyone will have to interpret in their own life what is happening, if they are forever tripping over the same stone.

Last year, I listened to a talk given by the President of an important car manufacturing Company on human relations in his company. He talked about people in his company who were encouraged to progress, with the understanding that mistakes are part of the journey. He said, *"In our company we do not penalize people for making mistakes. We only penalize those who keep making the same mistake."*

Rule of the 3 Ps

Several years ago, a wine merchant from La Rioja, called Chivite, died. I don't know why, but I read the article that appeared in the newspaper the following day. I do not normally do it but, on this occasion, I did it because I read statements by his daughter who had spoken at his funeral. She spoke very proudly about her deceased father and of what she thought, above all else, was the guiding principle by which her father lived: the rule of the three Ps: Patience, Prudence and Persistence.

What we have been talking about is the last attribute: to be persistent to move ahead. Furthermore, we must have enough patience not to give up, while we make decisions with necessary prudence by considering the risks and benefits at each moment.

Sometimes moving forward means stopping

However, sometimes the way forward has to be looked at again. Moving forward may mean a change along our life's journey. If my *'moving forward'* is to complete my university studies within a specific time but suddenly, there is a sick family member, which requires me to take care of him or her, or the person who is providing my funding dies, I will have to change and perhaps delay the completion of my studies, or even abandon them in order to work to provide for the younger members of the family or for other reasons.

In this case, my '*moving forward*' will have changed and I will have to change and adapt. For some, it could involve '*putting a stop*' to this progress, but for others it could be to undertake what is important in life.

We are not in an era of change...

Increasingly, more people are saying that '*We are not in an era of change, but in a change of an era*'. Therefore, let us be clear that this change in an era requires leaders. It needs people to build a new and better era for all, and that we will only be able to do it if we are trained to Add Value. Therefore, wherever we see that there is an opportunity, let us contribute to the progress towards the change that is necessary in society.

SEVENTH AREA OF GROWTH: CREATE

"Inspiration exists, but it has to find you working"
Pablo Picasso

"Creativity is thinking up new things. Innovation is
doing new things."
Theodore Levitt

"A man with an idea is mad until he triumphs."
Mark Twain

"In moments of crisis, only the imagination is more
important than knowledge."
Albert Einstein

Seventh area of growth: CREATE

The action of creating or creativity is innate in human beings. There are some who do not feel creative; others do not think about it, they simply act and try to create everyday. Today, I have not come to talk about creativity that springs up spontaneously, but about the kind of creativity that emerges after a process of development or maturity. I cannot ignore the fact that it is a field that fascinates me most and as such I want to share a series of thoughts.

Create value

The driving force in our lives is the need to create, to add creativity to every moment and in every corner of the life that we have. We create new ways of relating to others, of resolving conflicts, studying, doing household chores, cooking by mixing different ingredients, when doing research, or at work when we use creativity to resolve problems or discover other more efficient ways to do things.

We are here precisely to bring about this creativity that will have an enormous impact in the future. Perhaps it is this area of growth - creativity - which is the major *leitmotiv* (recurring refrain) of today's message on Adding Value.

We are all creative people; and what is desirable is that we offer this creativity to others to improve what we find. We know that it will not always be an easy task, given that there are always people who put up barriers to change.

There are people or groups, within organizations, who specifically do not want anything to change or are simply afraid of change. I call them STATIC.

They are everywhere. We see them today and we will come across them often in life. What is important is that we are aware that they are there, and that we, as members of a group, want to create, want to change the existing *status quo*, however small that change is.

There will be occasions in which we will be able to avoid conflict with STATIC individuals, and others in which it will be necessary to take a stance against their argument because if we do not, it would kill creativity.

Experience 30: Special action in a simple environment

At Christmas 2013, my family and I, along with a family friend, spent a day visiting a friend who lives in a small village in the Pyrenees. Our friend, who was somewhat older than 65, is a shining example of someone who Adds Value in everything he does. And once again, he surprised me.

We took advantage of that day to go with him to one of his regular meetings with the people of nearby villages. It was a very small place. At the meeting, there were eight of us, around half of the number of participants. The age group of the other half was no less than 65.

Perhaps any other meeting of a similar kind in the village would have lasted a short time and everyone would have gone home at the end of it. But our friend, as he always does, spoke with a lot of clarity and expressiveness. At the end, he told them that he had brought them a gift. The surprise came when he handed out a sheet on which he had put together quotes from famous people, along with a great message for the occasion we were celebrating. Everyone knew that at this kind of meeting, this was not what was expected of a man above 60. The attention to detail had great value, and it brought great value to this setting and to those people.

What was certain was that he added value to me because, a week later, I had to prepare for a meeting of company directors from several countries at my company. To get across that we had to work harder to improve our business in the new environment of uncertainty in which we found ourselves, I included a quote which my friend had 'given away' a few days before.

The quote was from Hermann Hesse and it stated that, "In order to achieve what is possible, you have to try the impossible over and over again." My friend said it to several of us. I said it to several people. If each of us, afterwards, says it to others, we will be virally transmitting the 'gift' and, in this case, creating a viral transmission of something that adds value because it is as important to Add Value as it is to transmit it.

Train yourself to Add creative Value in everything you do.

As we said at the beginning, we have to train ourselves to Add Value. Things do not just happen spontaneously. If we do not train ourselves early and, moreover, if we are not aware that we are adding creativity to our actions, it will be difficult for us to measure, assess or even improve what we are *'adding'*.

When we perform professional duties as a lawyer, plumber, electrician, medical doctor, engineer, photographer or teacher, we must find new formulas to improve what we are doing, not only in the technical aspects of the job, but also in the ways in which we relate to others.

It is therefore very important to learn to create from the time we are undergoing training both in terms of our studies and in all other parallel activities we are doing.

Often, it is our own attitude that adds creativity to our relationships with others; and it can generate other examples that, through viral transmission and sometimes without anyone being aware of it, can help to change things around us.

Experience 31: A question of fashion

For a business course, I had to study the textile sector. It is something of which I have very little knowledge in my day-to-day work but, by studying it from a business perspective, I learned things that I did not know before.

There was an idea that had been transmitted in modern society, but I wondered how many people knew about it when it happened. It was an item on fashion that I did not know anything about. I wondered if the people who wore jeans with the bottoms rolled up, with the ankles visible, knew where that custom had originated.

What I learned in that course on the very history of the business was that it was a custom that was started by groups of young black people in the United States to commemorate their slave ancestors who had been captured and shackled around the ankles, and forced to cross the Atlantic Ocean to be sold as slaves in America. The custom spread to many people, who began to wear their jeans rolled up at the ankles, some out of conviction and others simply to follow the fashion.

This is an action that went viral and, in this case, became fashionable.

I was once a witness to an event, which is worth mentioning in this section.

Experience 32: Association meeting, breaking action
There was a meeting of the leaders of various youth groups of a Leisure Time Association in the assembly hall of the Association headquarters. There would have been some 40 people of 20 - 35 years of age. Presiding over the meeting were the President and Secretary of the association, sitting at a table located high up on a stage. The rest of us attending, sitting in rows as in a school, faced the front.

On the last point of the agenda that was being discussed, there were differences of opinion between the secretary and some of the participants. It was now late, past 21:30. Normally this kind of meeting ended earlier, but on that day, it was much later and there was still a contentious point to debate. The situation became very heated because of accusations made by some, while others started shouting and making criticisms, which was unpleasant for the rest of the participants. There was no end to the raised voices and reproaches among the people attending the meeting.

The other participants adopted different attitudes. Some distanced themselves from the shouting at the meeting and picked up a document to read. Others simply left the meeting. The remainder looked on at the people shouting, not knowing what to do as passive accomplices in a verbal conflict that no one knew where it would end.

Suddenly, one of the people got up from his seat and slowly made his way to the board at the front of the hall near to where the President and Secretary were presiding over the meeting. This made some of those who were shouting calm down for a moment while they watched the person walking. When he reached the board, he took up a marker and wrote. The participants became quiet and waited for him to finish writing because he was blocking the board with his body and they could not see what he was writing. When he finished, he turned around to face the participants, allowing them to read in the most sepulchral of silences: "IN THIS MEETING, THERE IS NO RESPECT."

The silence lasted for several seconds until the person who had written on the board addressed the whole assembly saying that there they were leaders of children and youth groups, and that they were responsible for setting an example with their behaviour to the children and young people that they were leading. He stressed that on that day, there were no children or young people to witness their behaviour and that they should all reflect on

> *whether that behaviour was appropriate. When he had finished talking, he went slowly back to his seat, while the others watched him in silence.*
>
> *The President shared with the assembly that what had just happened was a good wake-up call. Those who were arguing and shouting stopped being aggressive and the meeting continued with the customary friendliness and respect of other meetings until they were able to deal with the whole agenda and come to decisions together.*

"That's the way it's always been done."

Perhaps this is one of the statements that causes me the greatest unease when I hear it, mainly at a professional level, but also within the family and even in behaviour among friends.

When someone asks why a certain action or behaviour is done and the answer is *'Because that's the way it's always been done'*, that is when alarm bells should be going off for two major reasons.

The first is that it indicates that the person responding has not questioned the reason for his action or behaviour, which in turn leads us to question the rest of his actions or behaviours without realizing it, especially when issues of health and safety are at stake or when they relate to economic issues that affect others.

Secondly, because without being aware of it, he may be making the same mistake which may impact on people, machines or economic investments.

In the past, I have advised people preparing for job interviews or when they are looking for a new job.

I remember two interesting cases.

Experience 33: Advising a specialist candidate

A friend of mine, below the age of 30, was involved in a job selection process for a multinational company.

Two days before his final interview, we had a chat. I knew that he was a very good student, and that during his university years, without realizing it, he was 'training to add value' by working as a volunteer with great dedication and professionalism. In addition, in his early working career he was very well respected.

As his recent jobs had been in a specific industrial sector, he wanted to talk about what he had done in recent years at his interview. During the time I was his adviser, I conveyed to him that the company to which he was applying a job, wanted young graduates to work in different areas of the company. Despite saying to himself that 'he had always worked in a specialized area and that he knew it very well', he changed his approach. The post that they were looking to fill was for a generalist and not a specialist. He had already shown that he had a command of his area of expertise and worked very well in it. Until that moment, he had always done the same thing at job interviews, showing only his strengths in the area in which he was an expert. The challenge for him now was to show that he could also work very well in other areas of the company, because he was aware of what he could do, given that he had enough skills to be able to adapt.

Weeks later, they offered him the post, and afterwards, having worked many years in the company, he has been promoted to several departments and in each has been adding value.

Experience 34: Advising candidates: adapting to the role

The last case is a very recent one. It is about a woman, about 40 years old, married with two small children. She had been working in the same company for many years in a very specific job.

Her misfortune occurred when the company experienced financial problems and had to cut staff to reduce fixed costs to survive, as the money market was applying pressure to it because of its high debt and the business outlook for the immediate future was not good. The company decided to add her to the list of people to be laid off.

Some months ago, we met up for a cup of coffee where she told me that she had spent many months sending off CVs but not a single company had called her. She had not had any job interviews despite her perseverance and dedication. She allowed me to analyze her CV and we agreed that there were some aspects that she could modify.

In her CV, she indicated the name of the post that she had held over recent years. The problem was that, with the economic crisis that the country was experiencing, no one was offering any more posts in the sector in which she was working. So, what she had included on her CV was something that was no longer needed, and moreover, she had not realized why there was no more work in the field. The conclusion that we arrived at was to change what she had been doing in the last few months, not only in what she had written but also in her approach. The decision was to focus more on her CV, highlighting the duties she had performed and, more specifically, the skills she had acquired, which would allow her to add value in other sectors and jobs, rather than on the name of the job that she had done.

We met up again for a coffee a few weeks ago, and she told me that she was working in a company. It was a joy to hear that, after our last meeting and after she had sent a revised CV, literally, at least four different companies had contacted her. The first two, to which she had gone for an interview, had offered her a job and she had taken one of them. She told me that at the interviews, to show that she could do what they required, she had talked about her experiences in her last job (avoiding confidential issues), in which she demonstrated her skills, in particular, in negotiation, which the new company was looking for. Of course, she showed her ability to adapt to new working environments, according to what we had said at our first meeting, at which she herself had demonstrated that she had to undertake various projects in a changing environment.

So, clearly, adapting her CV had been crucial. We cannot send the same CV to various companies because we need to know beforehand which of our abilities, training and knowledge is more important for one company or for another. To sell a product, we must highlight features that might interest a customer. To sell ourselves in a CV and in a subsequent interview, we must highlight what we know best how to do and what may interest the other party. We can never lie. We must always know what they need, confirm that we have it within our abilities to deliver and highlight this above everything else.

On occasion, this sort of behaviour may be influenced by the leadership style of the group. In the family, if parents say to their children that they have to do something or other simply because they told them to do it, and when their children ask *'why'*, the response is *'that's the way it's always been done'*, then we parents have to question the response before making it.

We often encounter this sort of behaviour at the workplace. This is where creative minds looking to add value will question the continuation of this attitude. The very systems integrated within the quality management system at factories and, I know, also at schools, have revealed customs that not only do they **not** add value, but they actually **reduce** it.

In an actual case in an industrial company, when they applied quality management systems, it was discovered that they had been putting in twice the amount of additive that was needed to the final product at different times during the process. While the excess of additive did not compromise the final result, it was unnecessary. The problem was that it was **reducing** value, given that they were spending large sums of money on an unnecessary quantity of additive.

It is in responding to the title of this section - *that's the way it's always been done* - that we discover truly creative people. We must question why we do things, and our response should never be: "*That's the way it's always been done.*"

It is to creative people that I dedicate this story I read a long time ago in the book, *The Song of the Bird,* by Anthony de Mello. It always comes to mind when someone gives me this reply.

Reading

The Guru's Cat

Every evening when the guru was sitting for his meditation ritual, the cat of the Ashram would go around distracting the faithful. So the guru ordered the cat to be tied up during the evening's medication.

For a long time after the death of the guru, they continued to tie the cat during meditation time. When the cat died, they brought another cat to the Ashram to tie it during the evening meditation.

Centuries later, the disciples of the guru wrote learned treatises on the important role the cat played, as was only proper, during the ritual [17]

Be Linchpins

I cannot avoid making reference to one of the books I read recently: Linchpin: Are you Indispensable? (Seth Godin, 2010). The author draws a very interesting and important picture for anyone working in an organization or anyone who belongs to a group of friends or family members.

I focus on the title - *Linchpin* - chosen by the author because it represents the axis of a wheel. He invites us to reflect on the fact that taking on this role in our organizations can be very beneficial: to be linchpins in our groups. He proposed this idea from the perspective of uniting people and combining the energies, abilities and strengths of members and others to progress in the achievement of the objective of the organization.

In some organizations, how often do we encounter people who are extremely jealous about what they do and do not wish to share it with their colleagues? Sometimes it is because they fear that others will rob them of their job or sometimes it is because of their need for 'unnecessary' importance. The message for those people is that they do not realize that if they shared what they are proposing with others, it would be improved by them; and if they are in contact with different people, this would be the best way of using the different strengths of some and others to make progress and to create.

In fact, it was after I had started giving talks on Adding Value a few years ago, that I came across this book that invites everyone to *'Create Art'* in all that they do at work and within organizations. He invites us to consider ourselves as *'artists'* because each of us is capable of creating something new in everything that we do, both in our behaviour with colleagues as well as in the technical part of our work.

Experience 35: Creative mother - teacher

I know a person who, when her two children were 7 and 9, proposed something special.

She is an international financial analyst and speaks several languages. She had decided to take a break from her career as a director at various multinational companies to dedicate herself to her family for a designated period of time, with the intention of returning later to work when it was deemed convenient.

During that year she planned to boost her children's learning in French, and after mentioning it to other acquaintances, the children of friends joined her booster sessions which she ran on a purely voluntary basis.

She told us that at the beginning when she started these sessions, she had a lot of problems with her own children's attitude about being in a 'class' with this teacher who was in fact their mother. She thought about it for a while and found a creative way to solve the problem.

After she put it into action, not only her friends' children became more attentive, but also her own children became eager for the 'class' to arrive.

What she did was to become 'Madame Chocolat'. She stopped being herself, she stopped being the mother of her own children; instead she was this new character that she had invented. Madame Chocolat, of course, only spoke in French, wore somewhat eccentric attire with a small Eiffel Tower and the French flag as a pendant, behaved in a hilarious manner, with her own rules for her class and in beautiful French told them how much she enjoyed chocolate and how it was made.

This character attracted the children, not only to the French language, but also to French culture, since for her what was important in the teaching and learning of languages was to open the door to a new culture. With Google Earth, they learned about the streets of Paris, they sought out the Seine river, the Gargoyle of the Notre Dame Cathedral and the Moulin Rouge. They learned about how many countries in the world and in which ones French was spoken, they listened to popular French songs, they watched French films together, they ate chocolate and the prize at the end of the course was... to travel to France together. Everything was different, thanks to Madame Chocolat, even if she could not, unfortunately, go on the end-of-year trip... or could she?

Recognize the people who are creative

One of the ways to create and to be creative is precisely to recognize others who are creative, because one of slogans coming from Business Communication – in which many journalists work in public/private companies, NGOs and other organizations - is that *'what is not recognized does not exist'*.

Therefore, applying this to our own relations with work colleagues or friends, if we want something to happen, we must talk about it; if we want people or a group to continue to be creative, we must compliment them on their creativity.

It is as important to detect creative attitudes in people as it is to communicate it to them. Some people are instinctively creative; so if we are aware that they have had a *'Creative Moment'*, let us tell them so. If they are aware of their *'Creative Moment'*, it will serve to show them that we liked it; and if they are unaware, it will help them discover the *'creator'* within them.

In both cases, recognition can release an endless chain-reaction, like radioactivity when one atom hits two and then each of the two hits another two and so on. Let us be *'radioactive'* and let us through a little communication make *'creativity spread'* to *'increase creative actions'* and, in the end, change into a culture of continuous creativity.

Recognize that you too are creative. Be aware of those creative moments. Do not let yourselves be influenced by those who say that only a few people are creative. We are all creative, both artists and professionals in any branch of study; both father and mother who do special things with their children; as young people who influence their families with their creativity, adding value from one day to another, even if it sounds strange, and also in daily life.

They should make Creativity a subject for 17-year-olds and at university and non-university courses, across year groups, to make students more aware that what they are studying is useful and may open up different opportunities or, as I will explain later, look laterally at problems to find creative solutions.

Being creative means seeing things that can be applied to others.

This creative part of ours that we are talking about can be a unifying force: to combine different concepts to improve one of them, to bring together connections that exist between things and people, to combine knowledge of one thing to another to find new ways of doing things.

Sometimes I feel like a collector of experiences, my own and those of others, trying to see what can be used in the future if the same circumstances are repeated, what can be adapted from an initial idea if the circumstances are different, or even, knowing what not to do.

Creativity is about taking a plunge.

If we wait for our idea to be perfect, it is likely that by the time we put it into action it may never meet our expectations, or if it does, the idea may already have lost its relevance. Obviously, without proposing a naive, reckless or careless approach that could put the safety of people or things at risk, or even have a negative impact on our environment, creativity in itself has an impetus, of a lift-off that does not wait for the perfect moment.

In the world of the internet, this is perfectly understood. Many programs and applications are launched with minimal operational quality, but are gradually improved with *feedback* from users.

If we have an idea, it is very important to initiate it and not wait for it to be perfect before you launch it. Pass it around to others, your friends, companions, family members to our networks and see if it makes sense and if they like it. With the *feedback* received, improve it with everyone's help, transmit it and it will then grow.

Do not underestimate the power of the group or the community to build an idea to create. '*Communicate*', '*share*', '*improve*' are words that are implicit in creativity, and nowadays with the media we have, it is easier.

Lateral thinking

Although I am not going to talk about it at length, I cannot avoid making mention of one of the great gurus of Creativity. I refer to Edward de Bono who, in his book on <u>Lateral Thinking</u> (1999), explains that, in order to find creative solutions to some problems, we should avoid looking only at the problem directly, but opt to consider it from another perspective, to look for another way that has not been used before.

It is a book that should be on the reading list for all young people from the age of 17, and to be re-read periodically throughout one's life (perhaps every 10 years?).

Experience 36: A question of toys

I know a couple with three children. When the children were small, one of the issues that caused some irritation was that the children kept leaving their toys lying around the house. The more the parents told them not to do it and to put away the toys after playing with them, the more they would find small dolls in the most unsuspected of places - in the bathroom, or pieces that they would sometimes trip over in the corridor. The parents ended up picking up the toys and putting them away.

What's more, they realized that the toys being left lying around were not being used because they were not really playing with them.

First they tried peaceful means to get them to put away the toys, then they tried scolding and punishing them when they continued to be untidy. Nothing worked.

They came to realize that they were looking at the problem too directly: blaming the children for the disorder.

After discussing it between themselves and, applying Lateral Thinking techniques, they agreed on a new strategy. They put it into action and it worked.

The day after agreeing on the strategy, they bought a folding container some 70 cm high and 50 cm wide. They called the children together and putting the container in a visible place in the corridor, they told them that they were no longer going to punish them for leaving the toys lying around. Of course, the children looked on expectantly because they did not know if that was going to be good or bad for them.

The parents continued to explain that from that day onwards, they were going to punish the toys.

If they found a toy around the house and it was not being used, they would put it in the container where it would be punished for a week and they could not play with it. At the end of the period of punishment, the children could ask for the toy and they would give it to them.

What happened afterwards was that the toys that they liked, they took good care to put them away in an orderly fashion. The ones that they were left lying around, went into the box for 'punished' toys. When the week of punishment was over, the children no longer remembered those toys and the parents simply emptied the container into another box that was removed from the house.

Gradually there were fewer toys left around and the parents emptied the home of the ones that the children no longer wanted, but did not explicitly say so.

The era of creativity

It is so. There is no doubting it. The 21st century is going to be the century of creativity because, among other reasons, if it were not so, man would have great difficulty in overcoming the challenges he faces with regard to environmental issues, social imbalance, economic problems and the instability of world peace.

If we really believe this, and I am a fervent supporter of this statement, we should fully understand Richard Florida who, in his book *The Rise of the Creative Class* (2002), explained how he had expanded his research to include other parts of the world. According to Kotler et Al (2010), what Florida found was that *"European countries also have a high creativity index, which measures creative development of a nation based on its advancement in technology, talent and tolerance."*[18]

Experience 37: The benefits of a good recommendation

This is a personal experience.

In October 2014, I was at a bookstore at Barcelona airport looking for a book to read for the following weeks that I would be travelling. After watching me for a while looking at the books, the saleswoman approached and offered to help me.

It was pleasant to meet a professional like her who, in her role as a saleswoman, was trying her utmost to satisfy the needs of the customer. Her first two questions on the kind of reading I liked were not successful in helping me find something interesting. She listened to me, made sure that she understood me and showed great knowledge of the Literature she was selling, both in terms of their titles and their authors. Finally, she offered me a book from what they had in the shop. In the end, I bought it.

I often go back to that bookshop, but I have not seen the saleswoman who sold me the book. I am enormously grateful to her for three reasons:

The first is that she made me appreciate her job, her commitment, and how she was capable of adding value by selling me a book (I have to admit that it is no easy task to sell me anything).

Secondly, because of the book, <u>Prométeme que serás libre</u> (<u>*Promise me that you will be free*</u>)*, by Jorge Molist (2014), which I enjoyed very much. I enjoyed reading it on my business journeys during the following weeks. The only problem was that, despite its thickness, it took me fewer days to read it than I had expected to finish it.*

Finally, the book was interesting because of the biography of the author. To date, I have never spoken to

> *him. However, knowing that Jorge Molist had studied Industrial Engineering, then did his MBA, then worked at various multinational companies and, nearing his 50s, decided to write books, helped me.*
>
> *I suppose that I identified personally with him and the fact that I had started to write a couple of stories encouraged me to continue and to publish books.*

To reinforce the message of this small section, I have another quote. This one is from Danah Zohar in 1990, cited by Kotler et al in 2010. For Zohar, "*creativity makes human beings different from other living creatures on earth. Human beings with their creativity shape their world. Creative people constantly seek to improve themselves and their world. Creativity expresses itself in humanity, morality and spirituality.*"[19]

Therefore, if what we need is creativity in order to progress and to improve in this new era, then it is not I who will share the last experience with you.

Instead, I suggest a tribute to all those who have been able to create companies, organizations, NGOs, who have succeeded in being sustainable and have generated employment or wealth in deprived areas, or hope among users of their services, who have created and continue creating artistic works from literature, painting, cinema and photography, among others, and continue to seek that 'something more' in every step they take. I suggest you ask your friends, parents, acquaintances, and do research on every case where people have risked time and money to give work to others and manage it in an appropriate manner in order not to succumb to the negative impact of the present financial crisis. I suggest you ask and talk to people who have set up a firm of lawyers, a hairdresser's salon, a service company, an NGO, a Leisure Time Association, a book publisher, and a film producing company, or whatever it is that has generated sustainable employment. Let them tell you their experiences, how they formed it, how they overcame difficulties, the main ideas that they based it on and the incentives that motivated them. I suggest that you begin this analysis today. In the course of your lives, do not stop doing it for one moment. Discover how each of them has worked on the SEVEN AREAS OF GROWTH we have talked about today, to Add Value.

And the last suggestion is for you to be aware of your own experiences, reflect on them, compile them and share them. Perhaps in 30 years time you might be able to tell other young people, like yourselves today, if they are interested in building their future.

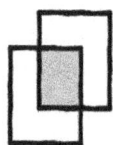

CHAPTER 9

He has finished.

He is looking at us.

He is waiting for something from us. He is waiting for us to say something.

No. He has not finished. He is approaching the edge of the stage, and looking at us fixedly, he begins to speak in a low voice.

"After all that you have seen up to now," the speaker continues, "in short, if we could sum everything up, we would have to talk about our mission to Add Value and create wealth in what we do in our studies, in our family, friends and in our paid or voluntary work."

"And if we consider the seven Areas of Growth to add the value that we have been talking about, we would say that it is an objective that puts us within a group, and manages our time and money resources to add wealth, and we do so with the aim of progressing each day with creativity."

Now, yes.

He has finished. I think he has finished.

In the room, there is only silence. We look at each other. There has been an avalanche of concepts and of experiences. He's said that all that he has told us are true. I liked it. I feel as if I were in a film at the cinema because he has managed to extract emotions and feelings from me. Many of the things he has talked about I have experienced at some time; and the link he had made with the book references is very interesting because I too do it. Every time I read in a book I have about what a character experiences or feels, I can see it from their eyes. But above all, I try to see if I could put something that I have read into practice in my own life. I like to dream, but more than that, I like to imagine myself doing incredible things.

I look at my friend sitting next to me, who asks me:

"Did you like it?"

I don't know what to answer her, because if she did not like it, or if no one else did, I will look strange. But if, on the other hand, everyone thinks the same and nobody dares say what they are really thinking, then we'll never know. I answer:

"Yes."

I observe the look of relief on her face. So I do not wait for a second more to launch into my question.

"And you?"

"I loved it!" She answered, smiling broadly.

The two of us turned to look in front when we hear the speaker.

"I hope that you have all enjoyed it a lot, or more, that you have enjoyed what I have done in preparing this experience," the speaker begins, "and before we move on to questions, let us continue on to the final part of today's talk.

He again gets our attention because he goes to the computer where he manages the slide presentations appearing on the screen and we see that he has prepared the start of a video. We can see that image typical of a horizontal triangle pointing to the right, with the image frozen, waiting for a click on the mouse to start. The image behind, filling the screen, is a half-full glass of water on a table.

What surprises us most, my friends as much as me - we are leaning a little further forward so that we would not miss a detail of what he is doing - is what he does afterwards. He goes to the table where he has the computer. There, we have all seen the half-full glass of water during the whole talk. We have seen that he has not used it throughout the presentation. It continues to have the same level of liquid. Now, he holds it up, looks at us and says:

"To finish, I am going to show you a video which, for me, covers many of the areas that we have talked about today, and above all, it suggests a behaviour in our proposal to Add Value continuously. I am showing you what my 13-year-old daughter did for a Christmas video competition at her school. The video lasts no more than a minute at most.

We see him operating the computer and clicking on the mouse. The video starts.

CHAPTER 10

I don't know if I should have mentioned my daughter. I might seem somewhat snobbish, but as I am so proud of the work she did, I cannot prevent myself from talking about it. What I will not say to them is that, at her school, her video was the only one selected for a talk by one of the teachers in the hall with all the students.

I shall never tire of seeing this video, not even when I am as exhausted as I feel now. I have finished the talk and they have not asked any questions. I have scrutinized their faces to detect if they are bored or if they do not like it. I have not detected any sign of either, but that does not mean that there isn't. Now they seem even more attentive with the video from the moment I clicked the computer to start it.

I watch their faces while they view the text that appears horizontally across the screen, moving up from the bottom of the screen to the top and disappearing at the top of the screen.

HAVE A SIMPLE LIFE
APPRECIATE WHAT YOU HAVE

The text has come to an end and now they can only see the glass of water on a table with a neutral background at the end. The on-off voice of a girl is heard, saying:

"Dad, can I have a glass of water, please?"

After a second, the man's voice is heard. I imagine that they realize that it is mine:

"There it is on the table, darling."

"Thank you." The girl's voice is heard.

The following action - the girl's hand appears on the screen, holding the glass. She takes it and it disappears from the screen. Seconds later, with nothing on the screen, the same hand returns it to the table, but it is empty.

Now, there on the screen horizontal letters are seen moving up from the bottom to the top of the screen, where they disappear:

HAVE A COMPLICATED LIFE

APPRECIATE ONLY WHAT YOU DO NOT HAVE

I can hear them talking to each other, without taking their attention away from the screen.

Now the same half-filled glass of water appears on the same table as before, in the same photographic background as the first photo. The same girl's on-off voice can be heard again, saying:

"Dad, can I have a glass of water?"

The same scene is repeated, in which a man's voice says:

"There it is on the table, darling."

Although it is the same girl, but the difference now is that the tone of her voice is altered and angry as she says:

"Dad, how can I drink from this glass if it is half empty? I do not want to drink from a half-empty glass. DAD, I WANT A FULL GLASS OF WATER!"

I observe some uncomfortable fidgeting among the young people until they watch the last image with the glass in the background and the superimposed text, on which they can read:

AND YOU, HOW DO YOU VIEW THE GLASS?

At the same time, they hear the on-off voice of the girl saying:

"You can see the glass as half-full or half-empty." There is a moment of silence. "You can decide to live a simple life, appreciating what you have." There is another pause.

"Or you can live a complicated life and appreciate only what you do not have. And you, what do you decide?"

The film comes to an end. They are looking at me. I go quickly to the front of the stage with the intention of not allowing them to relax. I have come to the end of the experience. I am aware that I must end with something that has an impact, something for them to think about and to leave with a smile.

"WHAT DO YOU SEE?" I shouted, raising the glass of water so that they can see it properly.

As usual, nobody answers. There is silence. And so, I repeat the question.

"WHAT DO YOU SEE HERE?" I repeat again in a very loud voice, with my arm outstretched and looking directly at each of them.

Some stirred and answered, with a certain amount of unwillingness and in a tired voice, while I watch the slight smile on their faces.

"A glass.... half full of water!"

"I don't hear you!" I responded, raising my voice louder. "WHAT DO YOU SEE HERE?"

"A GLASS.... HALF FULL OF WATER!" Most of them shouted, while they smiled at me.

I remain standing in the same spot. I remain silent. I watch them for a second, and to surprise them, I drink the water in the glass.

I again look at them, with my arm raised and now holding an empty glass. I shout:

"WHAT DO YOU SEE NOW?"

That causes uncertainty and surprise among them. They look at each other because they do not know what to say. Someone cracks a little joke which I did not hear, but no one is laughing because they are waiting. I think that I have created expectation. I allow silence to dominate the room and I finish.

"I see..." I stop for a moment. I observe them and then I look up at my hand. "A glass full of future. Yours, that of your teachers who are here with us, and my own."

I allow them a few seconds to smile and chat. I go over to the projector and change the transparency for them to see the last one I had prepared for today.

I watch them all and walk quietly to the front of the stage as I say to them:

"Thank you for your attention. It has been a pleasure to be here with you and to share this experience with you. If anyone has not filled in the part of the sheet you have for noting down new ideas, I apologize now because it means that I have not succeeded in reaching you.

If anyone has put down something and you find it interesting, I suggest that you send the idea virally as soon as possible via Facebook, Twitter, ...Share, distribute and spread the word. Fill Facebook, Twitter, social networks with what you liked, spread the idea, the message if you think that it is good news, because an idea that you, you and you..." I point to several of them, "consider to be good, if you do not spread it, it dies."

CHAPTER 11

He's not bad. He's managed to impress us and above all, make us laugh. I see that some people are applauding. I liked it. I watch the others and I see that they too liked it.

I like to see how people use the techniques that exist. A few days ago, at a course for camp leaders for which quite a few of us had put our names down, they told us about the 'Animation Curve'. I would never have imagined that it could be used in a talk, as this speaker has done.

He made a strong start, raising the curve of the graphic that the course instructor was talking about the other day. He made us more attentive and increased our enjoyment of the talk. Halfway, he relaxed a little with some concepts that may be less attractive. In the last part, he succeeded in raising our interest with the PROGRESS and CREATE Areas of Growth. I think that the last one really appealed to us. Finally, he used the Animation Curve technique, increasing our attention even further and the development of the talk with his daughter's video and, of course, the glass of water.

While I watched and listened to him, I felt at times that I could identify with him because I too consider myself a collector of experiences to consider in the future. This summer, I'm going to work as a summer camp leader at a summer camp with 6 to 10-year-olds, and I am getting ideas for using the Animation Curve.

How many ideas! I had intended to relax in the last hours on Friday, but this man has achieved the opposite. I am anxious. I do nothing else but think about what he has said.

We are all leaving, as always, packed together in the Hall. We make our quick goodbyes because it's Friday and each of us is in a hurry to get home. I meet the two boys and the girl with whom I walk home as we live in the same area, a half-an-hour's walk from school. We make signs to each other and then take the usual route home.

As we turned the first corner, one of the boys asked:

"Did you like the talk?"

I was deep in my own thoughts and I've just realized that it is the first time that we have walked this first section to the corner without saying a word to each other. If they are all like me, I don't blame them because I have not stopped thinking about what the speaker had said. I have not stopped comparing my two sisters and the lives that they have led up till now.

My middle sister seems to have built her life on the principles of 7 - 17. She is always positive. When she has problems she tries to find solutions and often, I see that she shares them with her partner or her group of friends. In fact, it is not rare for her to come and eat at home with our parents and talk about a situation she is experiencing to hear other points of view.

Now I understand. Perhaps I had never noticed it before. Listen! It's true! I had never been aware before now of how my middle sister listens to others. She uses the ways that were described in the talk today.

Yes! If adults only knew that this is what we are really asking for every day and they don't realize it. I know that it is not just me because I've talked about it with my friends. From the time I was 13, I observed that they don't listen to me. They wait until we stop talking, if they haven't interrupted us halfway to tell us what we have to do. I suppose they don't mean anything bad by it, but with their criticism, they try to guide us. But, most of the time, it's the opposite. They manage to bring our backs up and make us not listen to them. If only they would let us finish talking and try to understand what we have said!

I notice myself smiling and, embarrassed, I look around at my companions to see if they have noticed. It seems that they haven't.

"Yes, I did." The other boy answers. "I expected a boring session for the last session on Friday, but I very much liked hearing about the experiences of an older person as if he were in our position only recently."

I think of my eldest sister. Why is she so different from the other? It is difficult to understand it - how could two people with the same parents, the same educational background and same opportunities have such different lives? Sometimes, I wonder if the influence of the middle sister has had some negative effect on her. She is more of a loner. She does not like being in a group, and most of the time she only speaks about herself and her problems. Economically, she lives above her means since she took out a bank loan which she has not yet paid off. It means that she is very dependent on the day-to-day in so far as her expenses go. I see that she is unhappy. Fortunately, she has not stopped studying, she practises sport, she is very hardworking and that is where I am very sure that she is adding value.

In fact, out of the seven Areas of Growth mentioned in the talk, my eldest sister is excellent in the last one - CREATE. She is one of the most creative people I have ever met. As far as I can remember, since she was small, she would surprise us all with ideas that no one else had thought about. Analyzing the concepts presented in the talk, I think her challenge is to improve in the area of PROGRESS.

That's it. That is where she has to develop - to perceive fewer problems before doing things, recover quickly after failure and, of course, stop always justifying her limitations since that is preventing her from interacting with people or undertaking new ventures. From what I've heard some time at home, my eldest sister could not cope well when she failed an exam at school or at university. In contrast to my middle sister who, if she failed something, would use it as a learning experience to prepare for the next exam, my eldest sister became greatly distressed. It was very difficult for her to get over it and to find the strength to prepare for the next one.

For a couple of years now, I have discovered that my eldest sister is much more intelligent that my middle sister. Although, today, I should be saying more intellectually intelligent because, according to today's experience, what my middle sister has more of is emotional intelligence.

I cannot continue to be a passive witness here. I am going to reflect on it and try to help my sister, with great care of course, to discover the truths of the experience that we have had today.

"It looks like the rest of you didn't like it." The companion, who asked the first question, interrupted the silence. "Or perhaps, you can't stop thinking about it."

"You are right." I answered. "Sorry for not answering you. I can't stop thinking of some people I know, and what could have happened if they had experienced what we had today... ten years ago."

At last I am back in the present. I had been distracted, thinking too much about my sisters, and I am again aware of the true friends I have, about all that we have experienced together, about how each of us shares and although we are all different, I think that we have fully understood today's message.

I stop for a moment. I allow them to see me as a principal artist of a small theatrical production. I raise my hand to my mouth. I simulate drinking from an invisible glass. I lift and extend my arm out with my hand holding an invisible glass. When I see that they are looking at me, I say:

"I now know what I am going to do from now on: fill the glass of the future by adding value."

They look at me, and while bursting into laughter, they imitate the arm movement, first to the mouth and then extending it up and holding an invisible glass. At that moment, we all say it out loud:

"FILL THE GLASS OF THE FUTURE!"

We are so happy and laughing that we were close to hugging each other right there and then. Then, at that precise moment, I realize that I am near my home, I look at my watch and making a gesture to leave quickly, I take my leave:

"I'm going to run home, guys, I have a lot to study."

I wave goodbye and quickly leave them, knowing that they are part of today's group and that together we will have many opportunities to do great things.

Glen Lapson
COLLECTOR OF EXPERIENCES

APPENDIX 1

THE MARCH OF THE INVOLUNTARY VOLUNTEER

There was once a generous young man who was offering his services as a volunteer in an association committed to giving voluntary aid to the involuntarily disadvantaged.

[....]

As a volunteer, he was very willing, but not too much. He had undertaken to go to the association every Tuesday, Thursday and Friday at six in the evening.

At the association, they were very happy with this new signing because they needed his contribution as an economics student to manage the accounts which was in a mess (as in almost all associations).

This volunteer, who was volunteering for this and was not receiving a salary, appeared one Tuesday, but on Thursday, he had a tennis match that he could not possibly miss and on Friday, at the University cinema club, they were putting on a very interesting film that he could not miss.

The following Tuesday, the volunteer, involuntarily beyond his control, arrived an hour and a quarter late, and went to work with great enthusiasm. The following Thursday, he arrived only half an hour late and he was already working hard as an economist when he received a call from Yolanda: "Don't you remember that today is my birthday?" "Oh, sorry!" And leaving papers scattered all over the table, he rushed out. For the next three days, he arrived at the association on the dot because when he went on Friday, he saw a somewhat strange expression on the coordinator's face. It was two weeks later when he saw the advertisement of an intensive jazz dance course in the newspaper. With his interest in Afro-American culture, his solidarity with black people, their body expression, he informed the coordinator: "...It will not be for more than two weeks... Then, I will be able to contribute..."

Two weeks turned to five, but on Tuesday of the sixth week, he appeared punctually at the association. At the desk he normally occupied, there was an elderly lady with fine-rimmed spectacles of the type worn on the nose which allow you to see above them. "Good afternoon." "Good afternoon," responded the elderly lady, returning to her work.

The coordinator appeared at the door: "Hi let me introduce Rosalia. She's a retired accountant who has offered... Can you come a moment?" He took him to his office.

"Look, the situation with the accounts is urgent, and although sometimes she has to bring her grandson or her husband takes ill, she has more time."

"But, I am a volunteer..."

"Yes, yes... I have another role for you. We have a meeting of the heads of non-governmental bodies, NGOs, foundations, pious associations, charity associations, and

we have organized something that I think will interest you. Note down this address."

The following Tuesday, the volunteer went to the aforementioned address. While it may appear redundant, on the door of that house in Old Madrid, there was a sign: 'Association of the Involuntary, 2nd Floor on the right'. Confused, he was about to leave, when his curiosity got the better of him and he went up. At the reception, a girl was putting on her coat. "Hi, you are new, aren't you? Here there is a flyer for the Association," and she left. In the reception room, there were young and old people of all sorts, crossing the room, and coming and going. It read: "Association of the Involuntary. Foundation of the Union of Social Service Groups. Our objective is to offer different kinds of activities for those restless young people and adults who want to do something (but not too demanding) with their lives.

This association has a room with magazines, a video library, a room for informal meetings. There is no fixed timetable and no specific rules. You can come as often as you want and commit to any activity of your choice, even if your many occupations and contacts do not allow you to follow through on your commitment.

The advantages of this association are: a. you will feel a sense of fulfilment; and b. you will not bog down the action of organizations that work hard for serious causes in defence of the disadvantaged. Activities we can offer you...."

The volunteer thought that it was not a bad idea and was about to choose an activity from the wide list, but at that moment, he looked at his watch: "Oh, seven-thirty. Today they are showing the Oviedo-Osasuna match again on TV!"

And so he rushed off involuntarily.

Author: Martín Valmaseda
Reading, from Worksheets for Training Courses for CARITAS Volunteers (Spain), September 1997

APPENDIX 2

LIST OF EXPERIENCES

Experience	name
1	Meeting of young people
2	Personal Interview: the Mountain
3	Tents
4	Young person with home commitment
5	Recruitment Test - the points
6	The Last Samurai
7	Solving the Problem of Distraction
8	Basic quality in a job interview
9	Job interview - Silence
10	Difficulties in a subject
11	Skills in a different profession
12	Keep active during your studies
13	Job interview - Reading
14	Spelling
15	The best bosses
16	When to do sports
17	Question or situation
18	Personal Hygiene
19	Qualities of the 'Children of the Millennium'
20	The Consequence of lying
21	Special Teacher, Special Action

BIBLIOGRAPHY

Bach, Richard . Illusions: The Adventures of a Reluctant Messiah. Dell Publishing Co. Inc., New York, USA, 1977.

Bach, Richard. Jonathan Livingston Seagull. Macmillan Publishers, New York, USA. 1970

De Bono, Edward. Serious Creativity, Using the Power of Lateral Thinking to create new Ideas. The McQuaig Group, Inc., 1992.

De Mello, Anthony, SJ. The Song of the Bird. Lonavia, India, 1982.

Ende, Michael. Momo. Editorial Alfaguara, 1984

Florida, Richard. The Rise of Creative Class: and how it´s transforming work, leisure, community, and everyday life. Basic Book, 2002. (Reference found in Marketing 3.0 by Kotler, Kartajaya & Setiawan, John Wiley & Sons Inc., New Jersey, USA. 2010, p.18.)

Frankl, Viktor. Man's Search for Meaning. Translated by Ilse Lasch into English from the original: *...Trotzdem Ja zum Leben sagen: Ein Psychologe erlebt das Konzentrationslager (1946)* and first published in English by Beacon Press, Boston, USA, 1959.

Frankl, Viktor. *El hombre doliente* Editorial Herder, 2000 (Original title: Der leidende Mensch. Anthropologische Grundlagen der Psychotherapie, Verlag Hans Huber, Berna, 1984)

Godin, Seth. Linchpin: Are you Indispensable? Portfolio, USA, 2010

Goleman, Daniel. Emotional Intelligence, Bloomsbury, London, UK, 1996.

Hagstrom, Robert G. The Warren Buffet Way. John Wiley & Sons, Inc. 2000.

Kabani, Shama. The Zen of Social Media Marketing (Third Edition) published by BenBella Books, 2013

Kiyosaki, Robert T. and Lechter, Sharon L. Rich Dad, Poor Dad. Warner Business Books, New York. USA, 2000

Kotler, Philip; Kartajaya, Hermawan; and Setiawan, Iwan. Marketing 3.0. John Wiley & Sons, Inc., New Jersey, USA, 2010.

Mandino, Og. *El vendedor más grande del Mundo* (The greatest salesman in the World), Random House Mondadori S.L.,1993.

Molist, Jorge. Prométeme que serás libre, Grupo Planeta, 2014.

Noiville, Florence. I went to business school and I apologize. Stock, Paris, France, 2009.

Otero, Herminio. Posters con Humor (Posters with Humour). Editorial C.C.S., 1982.

Rovira, Alex and Trías de Bes, Fernando. La Buena Suerte. (The Good Luck) Ediciones Urano, 2011.

Schein, Edgar H.. Organizational Culture and Leadership. Jossey-Bass Inc. Publishers, San Francisco, USA, 1985.

Yunus, Muhammad. Banker to the Poor - Micro-Lending and the Battle against World Poverty. PublicAffairs, 1999. (Vers un monde sans pauvreté. Editions Jean-Claude Lattrês, 1997).

Zohar, Danah. The quantum self: human nature and consciousness defined by the new physics. Quill, New York, 1990. (Reference found in Marketing 3.0 by Kotler, Kartajaya & Setiawan, John Wiley & Sons Inc., New Jersey, USA, 2010, p.19)

NOTES

[1] **Otero, Herminio.** *Posters con Humor,* Editorial C.C.S. 1982. p 59
[2] **Otero, Herminio.** Javi´s Drawing, Ibid., p 41
[3] **Frankl, Viktor.** *El hombre doliente,* Editorial Herder, 2000 (Original title: Der leidende Mensch. Anthropologische Grundlagen der Psychotherapie, Verlag Hans Huber, Berna, 1984), p. 59
[4] **Frankl, Viktor.** *El hombre en busca de Sentido, Editorial* Herder, 2003 (English text: *Man's Search for Meaning*, 1946), p. 155
[5] **Bach, Richard.** *Illusions*, 1977, Electronic PDF format: http://www3.cs.stonybrook.edu: p 11, No. 31.
[6] **Kabani, Shama.** *The Zen of Social Media Marketing*, BENBELLA BOOKS, INC., Dallas Texas, 2013, p. 110
[7] **Godin, Seth.** *Linchpin, Are you Indispensable?* Portfolio, USA, 2010, p 66 – 67, p 76.
[8] **Schein, Edgar H.** *Organizational Culture and Leadership*, Jossey-Bass Inc. Publishers, San Francisco, USA, 1985, p 29, 33, 35, 38, 40 & 43.
[9] **Mandino, Og.** El *vendedor más grande del Mundo* (The greatest salesman in the World), Pergamino 10, Random House Mondadori S.L.,1993, p 113.
[10] **Kiyosaki, Robert T. and Lechter, Sharon L.** *Padre rico, padre pobre*, Editorial Aguilar 2011 (*Rich Dad, Poor Dad*, 2008), p. 68
[11] **Kotler, Philip; Kartajaya, Hermawan; and Setiawan, Iwan.** *Marketing 3.0*, John Wiley & Sons, Inc. New Jersey, USA, 2010, p. 103.
[12] **Noiville, Florence.** *Soy economista y os pido disculpas,* Deusto Grupo Planeta, 2011 (English Text: *I went to business school and I apologize*, Éditions Stock, Paris France, 2009), p 45.
[13] **Noiville, Florence.** *Ibid.*, p 74.
[14] **Rovira, Alex & Trías de Bes, Fernando.** *La Buena Suerte* (Good Luck), Ediciones Urano, 2011, p 40
[15] **Bach, Richard.** *Illusions*, 1977, Electronic PDF format: http://www3.cs.stonybrook.edu: p 50
[16] **Bach, Richard.** *Jonathan Livingston Seagull,* The Complete Edition E-book, Simon & Schuster, 2014: https://books.google.com/books?isbn=147679331X: p. 84.
[17] **De Mello, Anthony SJ.** *The Song of the Bird*, The Guru's Cat, 1982, www.arvindguptatoys.com/arvindgupta/songofbird.pdf, p18.
[18] **Florida, Richard.** *Marketing 3.0*, by Kotler, Kartajaya & Setiawan,

John Wiley & Sons, Inc., New Jersey, USA, 2010, p.18
[19] **Zohar, Danah.** *Ibid.*, p.19

www.ingramcontent.com/pod-product-compliance
Lightning Source LLC
Chambersburg PA
CBHW022037190326
41520CB00008B/613